"The Church of Jesus Christ gl[...] sion in this immediate season of two to three years will determine our readiness to address the share each of us will have in the coming century? All of us face decisive issues. We must determine how we will answer God's personal call on each of us and how we will steward the gifts and assignments He places before us.

"It is into these issues and others currently related that Barbara Yoder speaks with prophetic clarity, insight and passion. All three of these traits are honed by an integrity in life and leadership that distinguishes her and verifies her trustworthiness as a true leader for such times as these.

"I am pleased to commend this book to people at all points in life—business or church leaders, youth or adults, housewives or executives, believers or unbelievers. All will benefit from the wisdom and prophetic guidance offered by this woman who has devoted herself as a true servant of God for humanity."

—**Jack W. Hayford**, president,
The Foursquare Church; chancellor,
The King's College & Seminary (Los Angeles, CA)

"No matter what your denominational background, Christians agree that the world is turning upside-down as global economic and political systems are going through unprecedented upheaval. Barbara Yoder reminds us that often the dark night of the soul is internal, too—and that God's glorious power is at work during the earthquakes and hurricanes of life in as profound a way as when the sun shines on our lives and ministries. Barbara reminds me that God's presence during my hour of trouble is tangible, mysterious, prevailing and profound. Her passionate pursuit of the Father spurs me on in my day-to-day wrestling with God when the enemy whispers, 'Just quit!' And as I cling to truth when I cannot find my way in the dark, the awareness of His presence breathes fresh hope into my life."

—**Carol Kent**, international speaker; author,
When I Lay My Isaac Down and *A New Kind of Normal*

"Barbara Yoder has created a personal revival handbook for every serious Christian. *The Overcomer's Anointing* is like Extreme Makeover: Spiritual Edition. We have all had times in which we feel doubts about our faith. The darkest times in our lives seem to shake our foundations, yet we try to put on a façade of spirituality that does not match our internal spiritual barometer. *The Overcomer's Anointing* presents us with steps and encouragement toward personal victory. If each of us takes the responsibility to work through Barbara's blueprint, the combined efforts of Christians would bring a revival unlike anything the Church has experienced to date. Barbara Yoder's message is more than just words; it is life-giving food for the soul. You need this book. I know I do!"

—**Bishop Harry R. Jackson Jr.**, senior pastor,
Hope Christian Church (Washington, D.C., area);
founder and president, High Impact Leadership Coalition

"Writing from a base of personal experience and biblical truth, Barbara Yoder addresses a challenge everyone faces in life: darkness. Insurmountable trials, tough circumstances, relentless troubles, the dark night of the soul . . . these are dark times that we need to know how to navigate. You will receive fresh hope for the victory that awaits you on the other side. Having faced the darkness in your own life, you can then speak to others in the midst of their darkness. A timely and encouraging book!"

—**Jane Hansen Hoyt**, president/CEO, Aglow International

"Most people either dread or try to avoid seasons of darkness in their lives. With marvelous insight and her extraordinary ability to communicate, Barbara Yoder has taken on the task of helping us understand and embrace the dark night of the soul. She reveals God's redemptive process that takes our times of darkness and creates new things. As we emerge from these seasons, an anointing comes forth that shapes our sphere of assignment. I highly recommend *The Overcomer's Anointing* for anyone attempting to understand and overcome times of loss, confusion or any other challenges associated with a dark season in life."

—**Barbara Wentroble**, president and founder,
International Breakthrough Ministries;
president, Breakthrough Business Network;
bestselling author

"Dark times of the soul can confuse, isolate and bring anguish. Thankfully God's Word provides answers for troubled times. Barbara weaves these answers honestly and compassionately into these pages. As you read them, let hope take back the night. Meditate on them, and the overcomer's anointing will rise up, proclaiming, 'My best days are not in the past; they are in my future.'"

—**Dr. Tim Sheets**, apostle, The Oasis,
a CityGate Church (Middletown, OH)

"During unprecedented times of shaking in the earth, *The Overcomer's Anointing* offers perspective, hope and strategy for believers to live in victory in the midst of challenging days. Barbara Yoder does a masterful job of helping us navigate the season of darkness to emerge into the light of our new day. Each reader will be inspired to embrace God's purpose of transformation, personally as well as in the nations and systems of the earth, for His Kingdom to come in new and powerful ways."

—**Jane Hamon**, apostle and co-pastor,
Christian International Family Church (Santa Rosa Beach, FL)

"If you are walking through a difficult season, this book will not only give you hope that the dark time will end, but also the understanding and keys to move into your new season. I recommend it!"

—**Joy Strang**, CFO, Strang Communications

THE OVERCOMER'S ANOINTING

God's Plan to Use *Your Darkest Hour* as Your Greatest Spiritual Weapon

BARBARA J. YODER

Chosen

a division of Baker Publishing Group
Grand Rapids, Michigan

© 2009 Barbara J. Yoder

Published by Chosen Books
A division of Baker Publishing Group
P.O. Box 6287, Grand Rapids, MI 49516-6287
www.chosenbooks.com

Printed in the United States of America

Library of Congress Cataloging-in-Publication Data
Yoder, Barbara J.
    The overcomer's anointing : God's plan to use your darkest hour as your greatest spiritual weapon / Barbara J. Yoder.
       p. cm.
    Includes bibliographical references (p.   ).
    ISBN 978-0-8007-9455-2 (pbk.)
    1. Success—Religious aspects—Christianity. 2. Suffering—Religious aspects—Christianity. I. Title.
    BV4598.3.Y63 2009
    248.8'6—dc22   2009003665

Contents

Foreword

The key concept of overcoming is simply this: Find a way to win, do not be defeated, and advance into the fullness of your God-given destiny.

This book will help you understand the concept of victory and the importance of not giving in to the power of defeat. In a world filled with crisis and turmoil, Barbara Yoder's book is a must to assist you on life's journey.

This is the time to break "hope deferred"! Proverbs 13:12 says, "Hope deferred makes the heart sick" (NKJV). Don't let loss overcome you. Loss can produce shaking. But it can also result in joy, change and resurrection power. We have been given the power to bind the accuser. *So bind the power of the accuser!* The enemy will taunt you about everything you have ever done wrong during traumatic times. You must overcome self-pity, doubt and unbelief.

This book will fill you with hope in the middle of darkness. Usually in the midst of our dark times in life, we find ourselves filled with trauma and loss. These elements hide in our very cells.

Trauma is like a snapshot from a camera. The picture of the trauma is stored deep in our brains. But the Holy Spirit wants to move in such a way that we are sovereignly delivered. He wants to give us a new perspective on life and the world around us.

Trauma also affects the very ground on which we walk. The enemy takes advantage of us during difficult times of loss or change to manipulate our emotions to create:

- A failure mentality;
- Confused perception of our lives and destiny;
- Dullness, deadness, lost hope or apathy in our "spirit man";
- Blocked emotions and
- A bitter root defiling the whole body.

When we do not deal with trauma effectively, we allow roots to grow that entangle our feet and keep us from moving forward on our new path of success. Trauma imprinted on our memory systems is also absorbed deep into the tissues of our brain (the processor) and affects our thoughts and our very hearts. Trauma becomes the "flashbulb" that determines what we see and how we define the world around us. When not processed correctly, trauma will shape your world from the point of view of the incident. Trauma can produce "lock-ins" of fear, failure complexities, emotional distress and anxiety, even causing our organs (spleen, kidneys, pancreas) to overwork.

Oh, my!

We may be going through a lot, but there is a way for us to overcome, to reverse the power of our dark hour and to advance into the very best that still lies ahead.

An overcomer defeats past trauma and gains new strength to venture into the next season with hope. Barbara helps us gain the perspective of an overcomer, and she gives great practical principles for overcoming.

In the midst of darkness, there is light. In the midst of light, there is sound. In the midst of sound, we find His voice. The power of His voice chops down the forest of confusion around us. The power of His voice creates a path in our wilderness. The power of His voice breaks the waters open and raises our heads above the waves of doubt, grief and despair towering around us. The power of His voice overcomes any strategy the enemy has developed to hold us captive in his chains of defeat.

My favorite saying in life is "But God!" This is a book that explains how to shout the phrase *But God! The Overcomer's Anointing* will develop a mentality in you so that no matter what circumstance you find intruding on your life, you can shout, "But God! He is the light in my darkness!"

Dark hours lie ahead, but an overcomer's anointing will break through and give you victory. Barbara Yoder is a friend who is an overcomer and who has now helped all of us overcome.

Dr. Chuck D. Pierce,
President, Global Spheres Inc.;
President, Glory of Zion International;
Harvest Watchman, Global Harvest

Preface

Barbara Yoder has blessed the Body of Christ with some wonderful truths concerning the times of light and darkness. By using Scripture, biblical examples and life experiences, she reveals that God accomplishes His work in the darkness as well as in the light. Barbara's honesty and transparency in sharing the things she has experienced in her life make these truths come alive.

I have known Barbara Yoder during the last 22 years of my 55 years of ministry. She is one of the most spiritual, real and mature ministers with whom I have had opportunity to work. Her writings not only give words of truth, but minister Holy Spirit attributes of revelation, faith and great encouragement. Life-giving truths are found in every chapter of this book. Every Christian who wants to understand how God works in our lives during the dark seasons as well as in seasons full of light should read it.

Barbara's quest to discover God's ways in the darkness and in the light reads something like little Christian's journey in *Pilgrim's Progress*. Barbara discovers the pitfalls that Satan sets for God's children, but the greatest truth she discovers is that God is just as much at work in her life—as well as ours—during the dark and dismal times as He is in the bright and pleasant times. She challenges every reader to become a voice for God and a forerunner for His purposes.

Thanks, Barbara, for your willingness to go through God's process and receive this revelation that will bless thousands of Christians around the world. May God bless you with even more opportunities to bless the Body of Christ.

Dr. Bill Hamon, Bishop,
Christian International Ministries Network;
bestselling author

Acknowledgments

When writing a book, I become acutely aware of every person I have ever been influenced by as well as the books and resources I have digested over the years. Many people have played a part in the formation of this book, from family (my brother, Dr. Burt Jones, and my sister, Patricia Franklin) who have lived with me through significant times of change (and pain), to friends who have been in the trenches with me, gutting it out together. The pastors in my church played a key part in the unfolding of my understanding that has formed this book—Ralph and Phyllis Carnegie, Rod and Margaret Allen, Brad and Lori Bandemer, Lynn Luelen, Tonya Roberson and Joyce Gamlin. I cannot forget Cindy Williams who is always at my side, helping to carve out the future with the state of Michigan. Then there is the whole gang of church members who, together with me, have forged this story, trudging through the dark to find the light.

Dotted around the continent are close friends who have walked the path with me, dialoguing, ideating and encouraging, as well as stumbling in the dark with me to find the light of the new day. To all of these people, I am eternally grateful. And to God belongs all the credit. I never cease to be amazed at how He takes the difficult, the painful and the seemingly hopeless things and weaves them together to form the tapestry of an incredible story of grace.

Kathryn Deering has been an editorial godsend, helping me transform rough drafts into polished works of expression. Jane Campbell has become my editorial hero, excellent in her gift and wonderful in her personhood and at times incredibly funny. To all those unsung heroes who have played some part in making this book possible, I say thanks.

To my ministry heroes whose lives I watch because you keep me grounded, hopeful, future-focused, expectant and supernatural, always moving through the "stuff," reaching for the greater: Bishop Bill Hamon, Dr. Chuck Pierce, Drs. Peter and Doris Wagner whom I love and admire. To my original spiritual mentor, Patricia Beall Gruits, still a significant part of my life, I say thanks for paving the way before me.

I owe a debt of gratitude even to those who have served as sandpaper in my life. For it is often through them that my challenge comes, compelling me to find the new day and move to higher ground. I find no offense, no hurt, no bitter feelings, only gratitude for the push toward the higher place in God.

To all of you whom I have failed to mention—and there are so many!—my heart is full and eternally grateful. You have helped make me who I am and this book what it is. Thank you from the bottom of my heart.

1

The Challenge of Darkness

Remember when you were a little kid? At a certain age, almost every child is haunted by the idea that a monster or a bogeyman might be under the bed. You were sure you heard a little noise! You thought you saw something move! You could almost see those scary eyes and big teeth, along with the octopus tentacles slithering up onto your pillow. "Mommy! Daddy!" you cried out, and sometimes you ran to find them. Somehow they could always take care of the bogeyman!

The church that I pastor loves to pray. Several years ago after a prayer meeting, two intercessors returned to our church building late one night to retrieve their cars and go home. But in the darkened parking lot, they thought they saw an evil, demonic being. They freaked out.

What did they do? They did what they had learned to do as kids whenever that old bogeyman lurked in the dark—they fled. They jumped into one of their cars and drove a couple miles—to *my* house.

It was midnight, and they were scared out of their wits. I had difficulty persuading them to go back to the church without me. However, since I was not about to get dressed and drive to the church at that time of night, I got up and coached them about how to approach the situation. I rehearsed some Scriptures with them—what our authority is because we are seated in heavenly places with Christ Jesus (see Ephesians 1:3; 2:6), and how we are to rule and reign with Christ (see Revelation 5:9–10). We also looked at James 4:7: "Resist the devil and he will flee from you." The demon they encountered was real; but when they faced him with Jesus' authority, he had to run away. The bogeyman was a paper tiger.

When it was my turn at a later date to face another sort of threat, I was not so bold. Visiting a rural part of Africa, I traveled to the middle of a region where witchcraft was practiced prominently. On a black, moonless night, as I walked by myself from the evening meal to my room in another building, I found the spiritual atmosphere—enhanced by the pitch-dark blackness—unnerving. The slightest movement in the surrounding bush was enough to make me jump nervously.

At a meeting earlier in the day, a pastor had told me about the python snakes that lived in the bush around my location. He said those snakes were capable of eating cows. Walking alone that night, my eyes got as big as saucers as I tried to penetrate the darkness. If those pythons could eat cows, they could eat me!

Great woman of faith that I am, I skittered back to my room in record time. Needless to say, the threat was all in my mind. Bogeymen may be paper tigers, but the darkness masks that fact.

Night Light

In a *KAIROS* magazine article entitled "The God Who Hides in Darkness," Robert Stearns wrote about our instinctive fears:

> I have a five-year-old son, so I'm well aware of the need to turn on the night light before sending him to bed. . . .
> We tend not to like the dark. We frequently complain when we feel we are in the wilderness of a night season, as the psalmist does in chapter 139:11 [NASB]—"I say, 'Surely the darkness will overwhelm me, and the light around me will be night.'"

Darkness unnerves us, but God does not seem to see it the same way. Continuing with Psalm 139:12, Stearns points out:

> "Even the darkness is not dark to You, and the night is as bright as the day. Darkness and light are alike to You."
> God is total, complete, perfect light. He *is* light (see 1 John 1:5). When you *are* light, apparently no darkness is dark to you. If darkness and light are alike to God, then there must be a reason outside Himself that He would opt for one over the other. We can hereby deduce that when God chooses to drape Himself in darkness, it is not for His benefit, but for ours.[1]

Yet we remain afraid of the dark. We do not like to face the unknown. We would much rather be able to turn on the lights and find that there is no bogeyman after all, or at least obtain the advantage of seeing our enemy clearly.

This book is not about monsters under your bed. It is about the very real struggles we face when "the lights go out" in our personal lives, our dark times when we face insurmountable challenges, tough circumstances, relentless troubles. When our darkness has a spiritual element, we sometimes call it a "dark night of the soul."

This book is about the darkness, but it is also about the light. Specifically, it is about how the Light of God always, always, *always* prevails. The darkness cannot overcome it (see John 1:5).

You see, God is not afraid of the dark at all. He is not one bit intimidated.

In fact, the first place He appeared in Scripture was in the middle of darkness. He clothes Himself with it, hides in it and speaks in and through it. You could even say that God loves the darkness:

> The earth was without form, and void; and darkness was on the face of the deep. And the Spirit of God was hovering over the face of the waters.
>
> Genesis 1:2

> He bowed the heavens also, and came down
> With darkness under His feet.
> He rode upon a cherub, and flew;
> And He was seen upon the wings of the wind.
> He made darkness canopies around Him,
> Dark waters and thick clouds of the skies.
>
> 2 Samuel 22:10–12

> Clouds and darkness surround Him;
> Righteousness and justice are the foundation of His throne.
>
> Psalm 97:2

> Moses drew near the thick darkness where God was.
>
> Exodus 20:21

I invite you to explore the darkness with me. Regardless of how thick and black your darkness is, we will find God there.

When you and I come to understand the darkness from God's viewpoint, we will no longer be like little children, afraid. We will begin to see where Jesus is in the dark of the night. We will be able to follow Him into the light of a new day. Ultimately, we will shine out as lights in the darkness ourselves; we will become beacons of light to a society that is becoming increasingly darker; a society that is losing its ethical and spiritual mooring points and is wandering in darkness. I talk about this at length in my book *Taking On Goliath.*

God invites us to enter the darkness, even the dark night of our souls, so that we can overcome it. Of course it seems a little risky, and it may well be uncomfortable. But as astronaut Sally Ride said, "All adventures, especially into new territory, are scary."

You and I belong to the Lord of Light. Even when He allows seasons of uncertainty and chaos to plunge us into what seems like the deepest darkness, He will help turn our seeming setbacks into surrender, and victory will be within our grasp.

What Does Darkness Mean to You?

I asked the participants in a recent class I taught to tell me what the word *darkness* conjured up in their minds as it related to them personally. They mentioned fatigue, oppression, loss of direction, fear, confusion, the presence of evil, despair, struggle, depression, hopelessness, intimidation, fear of the unknown, anger and more.

The meaning of the word *darkness* is multifaceted. Let's look at a few of its meanings:

Darkness can mean the absence of reception, reflection, radiation or transmission of light. When depression, oppression, disappointment or sin visits you or me, we ask each other,

"What happened to your *face*?" Why? Because we observe that in dark times, something is missing or changed in someone's face. We look into each other's faces for clues. In better times, our faces reflect God's nature.

God asked Cain why his countenance (the expression on his face) had fallen. God observed that Cain's face had become darkened in some way. It no longer radiated the nature of his Creator, God, but rather the nature of Satan, the father of sin.

> Cain brought an offering of the fruit of the ground to the LORD. Abel also brought of the firstborn of his flock and of their fat. And the LORD respected Abel and his offering, but He did not respect Cain and his offering. And Cain was very angry, and his countenance fell.
>
> So the LORD said to Cain, "Why are you angry? And why has your countenance fallen? If you do well, will you not be accepted? And if you do not do well, sin lies at the door. And its desire is for you, but you should rule over it."
>
> Genesis 4:3–7

What does your face reflect these days? Do you look grim and tense? Has anyone told you what you are reflecting to others?

Darkness can mean wholly or partially black. Just as a black hole in space swallows everything around it, black absorbs all the colors but reflects none. The darker something is, the less it radiates—and the more menacing it seems.

While writing, I am staying at a condo on the Emerald Coast beach in Florida. Gazing out over the balcony, I see the darker water of the Gulf of Mexico contrasted against the white sand. It is easy to see that the sand reflects daylight, or even artificial light, better than the deep water reflects it. Dark water, dark forests, dark buildings, dark faces—all convey a threat, a risk, a challenge, a mystery. What is going on in a place that feels cut off, stifled, dangerous? It is too dark to tell.

We speak about a dark character or dark powers that lead to war. Was not Hitler's character dark—in other words, evil? A dark, evil power led him into war with much of Europe. Elie Wiesel wrote about the darkness that seemed to storm Europe during the Nazi era:

> Back then, the dark side of the human heart took over most of Europe. In the name of racial purity and absolute power, it turned hatred and violence into hungry gods eager for blood and death. . . .
>
> The greatest writers are incapable of describing what the Holocaust means. How to explain or even describe the terror, the prayers, the tears, the tenderness, the sadness of the scientifically prepared death of six million human beings? Six million young and old, rich and poor, scholarly and illiterate, strong and weak, religious and atheistic people. Six million human beings sentenced to death by an evil dictatorship not because of their faith or their circumstances but because of their very being.[2]

Darkness often includes evil. Consider your family, your neighborhood, your city, your country. Is it more light or more dark? In other words, how righteous is it, or how sinful and iniquitous?

For example, Haiti is the poorest nation in the Western Hemisphere, and it is certainly one of the darkest. Throughout the nation flows an undercurrent of evil voodoo practices mixed with Catholicism. Evil practices impoverish a nation and make it dark. Looking at the faces of the Haitian people (the adults, anyway), you can see that they reflect oppression. Too many Haitians look worried, hardened, impoverished and unhappy. Surrounded by evil, many of them practice idolatrous worship themselves. Haiti is not a blessed nation. As Psalm 33:12 says, "Blessed is the nation whose God is the LORD."

Years ago I visited Haiti. After only two days there, I was thinking, *Get me on a plane and take me home!* In order to remain in that country, I had to enter into prayer. I had to touch God so that His light could break in on my heart and dispel the darkness and oppression I felt.

Evil traits or iniquitous tendencies may run through your family like rats in a sewer. They are the family weaknesses, the tendencies to sin in certain ways. Consider Abraham, who lied about his wife, Sarah. Then his son Isaac later lied also. Iniquities are problems that plague a family for generations. They can include alcoholism, drug addiction, marital infidelity, abuse, rebellion and many other weaknesses or tendencies. These evils can cause families to display a dark side.

Darkness hides secrets. A "dark secret" is unknown to others. It is kept hidden in the dark. Secret societies such as the Freemasons hide dark secrets, practices and beliefs that keep idolatry in place and result in the lack of blessing for members and their families.

But nothing can stay hidden forever:

> No one, when he has lit a lamp, covers it with a vessel or puts it under a bed, but sets it on a lampstand, that those who enter may see the light. For nothing is secret that will not be revealed, nor anything hidden that will not be known and come to light. Therefore take heed how you hear. For whoever has, to him more will be given; and whoever does not have, even what he seems to have will be taken from him.
>
> Luke 8:16–18

Furthermore, God will deliver to us treasures that are held captive in the barrenness of dark and secret places. At some point in our future, God will release to us things we are not even aware of. These may be family members held captive by secret societies or by dark associations such as with Wicca and Satanism. God says in Isaiah 45:3, "I will give you the treasures of darkness and hidden riches of secret places, that you may know that I, the LORD, who call you by your name, am the God of Israel."

Darkness makes us destitute of knowledge, obscure, dim and spiritually or intellectually handicapped. God is filled with knowledge. He *is* knowledge. He is the One who has given us our minds, our ability to think and to process things mentally. He has given to each of us an intellect as well as a spirit. Both are supposed to be active and alive. As a matter of fact, James said that faith (a function of our spirits) without works (a function of our minds and bodies) is dead (see James 2).

God is wisdom, knowledge, discernment and understanding. These are not only spiritual qualities, but also natural ones. Because He created us with a makeup that includes spirit, soul (intellect, emotions, will) and body, we need to allow His light to shine into our darkness in all of these areas.

The prophet Samuel had a mentor, the high priest, Eli. But Eli's vision had grown so dim through the years that he could hardly see. His eyes were darkened (see 1 Samuel 3:2). Throughout the Bible, we find references to eyes so darkened that they cannot see, or truths so hidden that they are invisible. The Gospel itself is often hidden or veiled, darkened to the eyes of the beholder. We often say that one is "unable to see the light."

> But even if our gospel is veiled, it is veiled to those who are perishing, whose minds the god of this age has blinded, who do not believe, lest the light of the gospel of the glory of Christ, who is the image of God, should shine on them.
>
> 2 Corinthians 4:3–4

A Time for Darkness

Just before He was arrested, Jesus spoke to the angry mob who had ambushed Him in the night:

> Then Jesus said to the chief priests, captains of the temple, and the elders who had come to Him, "Have you come out, as against a robber, with swords and clubs? When I was with you daily in the temple, you did not try to seize Me. But *this is your hour, and the power of darkness.*"
>
> Luke 22:52–53, emphasis added

I think that is a very interesting statement: "This is your hour, and the power of darkness." Jesus knew what was happening, and He yielded to it. This time of darkness was on God's timetable. At any earlier time, when it might have been easier to arrest Him in public places such as the synagogue, His enemies could not lay a hand on Him. Now, however, they could.

There comes a time when God gives things over to the power of darkness, and this was the most important such time that had ever occurred. The Father gave His Son over to evil and to the power of darkness. Seemingly, He allowed the darkness to prevail.

But this time of darkness was only three days long, although all of creation held its breath, waiting to see what would happen. It seemed to take forever to go from Jesus' agony in the Garden of Gethsemane to His mock trial to His crucifixion on Calvary to His burial—and take even longer until Easter morning. The darkness was utter and complete, especially when He gave up His Spirit and the sun disappeared. Three momentous days of tumult and chaos were followed by eerie silence broken only by hopeless sobs. Yet in the grand sweep of universal time, it was like the comma in this sentence.

26

The Father gave His Son over to the evil power of darkness for that space of time because He was going to break that power. It was the most strategic moment in the history of creation.

We are living in a greater darkness than ever before. Every day, we face challenges many people before us never imagined possible in their childhoods—things such as terrorism, the loss of childhood innocence, a death-focused society, widespread drug use, broken marriages, abused children and television programs that mainstream sex, rebellion and anarchy. The list could go on and on. We face enormous threats both from within our cultures and outside of them. At times, the darkness is palpable. In the world around us, and often within our souls, we are walking in the dark.

As with Jesus in His darkest time, we know that our darkness, our dimness, our spiritual destitution, is not from God, and yet God is in it: "For it is the God who commanded light to shine out of darkness, who has shone in our hearts to give the light of the knowledge of the glory of God in the face of Jesus Christ" (2 Corinthians 4:6). God will bring us out of the obscurity of darkness: "In that day the deaf shall hear the words of the book, and the eyes of the blind shall see out of obscurity and out of darkness" (Isaiah 29:18).

What kinds of darkness do you see in your own life right now? Have you been blinded by the darkness and sin of the world around you? Are you being tossed to and fro as the political or financial climates change? Are you embroiled in marital or family problems that just will not go away, to the point that you want to jump ship sometimes? Are you confused, not sure where you are going, wondering where your former joy and peace went? Do the lights seem to have gone out in your life?

Created to Overcome the Darkness

Are you ready to start shining some light into your darkness?

Could it be that God is beginning to get your attention in a way that He has not had it before? Could it be that He is allowing desperation, anxiety, fear, harassment, despair, misery, anguish, even desolation, to arise in you to the point that you will be driven to your knees for answers? Are you asking questions you either evaded before or did not think to ask?

As bad as things seem, could it be that you are in exactly the right place at the right time?

God wants to do something new, something that will change you, your family, your church, your neighborhood, your city and even your nation. Perhaps you were unable to hear what He was trying to say or see what He was trying to show you, so He had to let you *feel* it. Perhaps this is His rallying cry so that you will arise and find answers to the problems.

He had to allow the darkness to surround you before He could create the new things in your life. If you do not believe me, just think of the dark, "secret place" of your mother's womb where you were formed. Just think of the Creation:

> In the beginning God created the heavens and the earth. The earth was without form, and void; and darkness was on the face of the deep. And the Spirit of God was hovering over the face of the waters. Then God said, "Let there be light"; and there was light. And God saw the light, that it was good; and God divided the light from the darkness.
>
> Genesis 1:1–4

This season is not a mistake. You are not lost in the darkness/wilderness permanently. And if, perchance, you are doing just fine, thank you, and darkness/wilderness is not even on your screen at the moment, please hang on to this book. You *will* need its message in due time. Dark seasons are part of the growth process for each and every disciple. When you gave Jesus permission to be the Lord of your life, you signed up for some significant challenges. You cannot be an overcomer if you do not have something to overcome. Reach out and accept the anointing to be an overcomer, one who radiates the light of Christ into the darkest places:

> Do all things without grumbling and faultfinding and complaining [against God] and questioning and doubting [among yourselves], that you may show yourselves to be blameless and guiltless, innocent and uncontaminated, children of God without blemish (faultless, unrebukable) in the midst of a crooked and wicked generation [spiritually perverted and perverse], among whom you are seen as bright lights (stars or beacons shining out clearly) in the [dark] world, holding out [to it] and offering [to all men] the Word of Life, so that in the day of Christ I may have something of which exultantly to rejoice and glory in that I did not run my race in vain or spend my labor to no purpose.
>
> Philippians 2:14–16, AMP

Let God pour out the overcomer's anointing on you. Through it, He can use your darkest hour as your greatest spiritual weapon. This is an awesome calling!

2

Behold, I Do a New Thing

One cold December morning, I was sitting in one of my favorite chairs with a hot cup of fresh coffee. As its warm aroma filled the air, I gazed out the window, drinking in the beauty of a snowy Michigan day. The trees behind my house stretched out their arms, inviting the powdery snow to fall on them. Christmas music was playing in the next room, and the fireplace crackled and popped as the flames skipped across the logs. I sat there for a long time completely contented, meditating.

I thought about what Ecclesiastes chapter 3 says about a time and a season for everything. Gone was the lush, green summer foliage. Gone were the flowers large and small. In their place was a blanket of snow, and the busy summer sounds had been replaced with a soothing, peaceful quiet.

I thought to myself, *This day is a special day*. I reviewed the past few weeks. My last trip had concluded a rigorous travel schedule. That trip had been very significant. Something had happened that had never occurred before. While I was preaching, an unusual explosion of the Spirit of God occurred in the meeting. It was touchable, real, substantial. It was as if God's presence had invaded the place, filling the auditorium. Thousands of people responded by rushing to the front of the conference center. I myself felt completely overcome by God. I could hardly stand. I did not know what to do with such an unusual degree of God's presence. It was stronger than I had ever experienced anywhere outside of a Kathryn Kuhlman meeting many years before.

What did this mean? As I stepped off the stage, I began to weep almost uncontrollably; not from grief or depression but from an encounter with the living God. I could not talk; I was dumbstruck. My hosts whisked me off to catch a plane. I wanted to talk with them, but I was unable to utter a word.

So there I was that December day a few weeks later, relaxing at home and pondering the happenings of the past month. I was still overcome, still quite emotional over what had happened. I could not get away from that experience. Not only could I not get away from it—something seemed to have shifted within me. It was as if I had been shot through with something like a bolt of lightning at the highest voltage possible, and it had internally rewired me.

As time wore on and the holidays passed, I began to recognize that something inside me had shut off. I was not unhappy; neither was I depressed. I did not feel particularly weary, nor was I burned out. I had taken plenty of time to rest. Physically, I felt refreshed.

Yet something seemed gone; something was lost. I simply could not locate the same drive, the same energy-filled vision that had kept me moving forward unrelentingly up to that time. It was as if someone had turned out the lights to the place I had been living. I had never experienced anything like this before. It was distinct, definable and significant, but also disconcerting. What in the world had happened?

I could only connect what I was experiencing to that incredible encounter with God. It was as if God was saying, by actually doing something within me, *I am creating a new thing. I am clearing the past, erasing your hard drive, delivering you into a new place, a foreign place, somewhere you have never been before internally. I am removing you from the old by shutting it off.*

Still overcome by God, I found I would momentarily choke up, teary-eyed, anytime, anywhere. Even in the midst of experiencing such an overwhelming sense of God's presence, I thought I would get back to what I had been doing with fresh vision, strength, desire and drive. But it was not there. I could not find the old vision.

No Way Back

December is always a more relaxed month than most for me. I seldom schedule any ministry trips out of town after the first weekend so that I can take time to catch up on my personal business, deal with work responsibilities, rest, visit with friends and take family time. Because of December's more relaxed pace, I did not realize that whatever had happened to me on my last trip was not going to go away. I thought I was extra tired, and I expected that the month of December would enable me to garner energy and passion for the new year. Not this year, however.

As January arrived, I was still wondering what in the world had happened to me. Though not struggling in any particular way, I had no desire to do what I had done before. Finally, because I could not sit and do nothing, I simply returned to my former activities. For the life of me, though, I could not figure this out. *I have always found my way before,* I told myself, *and this time will be no different—right?*

Wrong. Little did I know that I would *never* find my way back to who I had been and what I had been doing before. It was as if God had thrown a grenade into the former Barbara Yoder. My identity and my way of seeing things and activities were different. My old methods would not work anymore. I could not locate my previous passion for my work.

Somehow, as I returned to the things I had been doing all along, I found myself beginning to struggle. I wanted back what I now felt I had lost. I spent extra time in the Word and special times in prayer. I fasted, seeking and asking God what was up, all to no avail. Had God left me to myself? Did He know I was beginning to struggle? How was I supposed to figure out how to move forward? I had always been the type of person who moves forward toward a vision no matter how difficult things become. This perplexing time began to confuse me. Why? Because hardship or difficulties had not plunged me into this limbo-like place—but rather an unprecedented encounter with God put me there. And I could not find my way out of this internal nothingness.

Lord Chesterfield once said, "Man cannot discover new oceans unless he has the courage to lose sight of the shore." I had lost sight of the shore, all right. Now I was floating on a vast, indefinable ocean, with no land in sight.

Status Quo No More

God had cut off my mooring points. I remembered how He had declared again and again through His prophets of old (and through modern-day prophets, including me) that He was taking us into "a new day" and doing "a new thing." In Isaiah 42:9 He said, "Behold, the former things have come to pass, and new things I declare; before they spring forth I tell you of them." And Amos 3:7 declares, "Surely the Lord GOD does nothing, unless He reveals His secret to His servants the prophets."

God had been trying to tell me that He was going to do a new thing. I believed it. Yet I supposed He meant that He would do His new thing "out there" somewhere, changing the Church or spiritual structures or something. I had not realized that He meant He would do all this rewiring, reworking, renewing, refreshing and rebuilding inside *me*. I had not expected such a significant overhaul. Therefore, I just kept on trying to be the same as I had been before, doing the same things I had done all along.

It just became more puzzling as time went on. Why could I not seem to connect to things as I had before? Nothing identifiable was wrong. Everything was going great. The church I pastor had an ongoing momentum of God's glory and presence. It seemed as if we were entering our greatest hour. As the leader, I had never felt more empowered. This was the day the prophets had spoken so much about; I just knew it! In fact, the anointing had never been any stronger than it was now. We had great services, awesome services. The Word of the Lord was rich. The presence of God was powerful. God was at work. We would come away from each service thinking, *Wow!*

So what in the world was this thing I kept experiencing? When I got alone, why did I feel so empty and void? I did not have a clue. I was feeling my way in the dark. *God had turned off the lights to the old things, but He had not yet turned them on to the new.*

Any time lights are turned off, it sets a new dynamic into place. Darkness descends, and we can no longer see. In due time, our natural eyes accommodate themselves to the dark. The same process happens with our spiritual eyes; God begins to give us new eyes to see what He wants us to see.

In Moses' time, God gave the Israelites eyes to see, hearts to perceive and ears to hear. They had seen the miracles God performed with Pharaoh, yet when they journeyed into the wilderness, they did not perceive the true message of those acts of God through Moses—the demonstration that He was with them and for them, and that He would fight for them if they would move into His destiny for them. They definitely did not perceive the new things. In other words, all they did was look back at what they had lost. They did not look to the future to see what they would gain—that God had ordained a Promised Land for them to enter and possess. Their eyes were darkened. They were blind. It is the same with you and me. We are blind to the new until God opens our eyes.

God had to form new eyes within me to see the new things He wanted me to see. Otherwise, I would revert to using my old familiar methods and patterns. I would perceive things using my most recent season's "filter."

What does it mean to receive new eyes, eyes that see new things? It is different for each person. For me it meant that how I saw things changed. How I saw God, myself, others, my calling and my ministry changed, including a shift in my focus and relationships. I did not move away to a new place or resign the church. For some this might have been the result. But I perceived everything in a new way. What I had formerly done, how I had done things, whom I did them with, where I did them and when I did them all went through a radical transformation that is still unfolding today. It was as if one book closed and a new one opened. One era had ended. Another had begun.

Dave Sim, a writer and cartoonist from Kitchener, Ontario, made an interesting declaration about his artistic inspiration. He said:

> These are ideas. I could say that they just came to me, but it would be more accurate to say that I went to them. Ideas—and

36

new connections between ideas—lead you away from commonly held perceptions of reality. Ideas lead you out here. Ideas lead you into the darkness.[1]

Ideas are "new things." They are like seeds, which become something new when they are given a chance to grow. But first, seeds must be thrust into darkness. Otherwise, they cannot become what they are destined to be. Seeds must be planted in the ground and covered with soil. They must be buried in dark places. In the dark of the soil, a seed dies; it loses its original form and function. After a time hidden in the darkness, a seed breaks forth with a green sprout of new life, promising eventual fruitfulness.

Conceived in Darkness

It is simple—to conceive the new in us, God thrusts us into darkness. So it is with birds, animals and human beings. All are conceived and developed in darkness, within an eggshell or the womb of their mother. Therefore, when darkness comes over you, you can be sure that God is making something new, because His new things are always conceived and developed in darkness.

As I mentioned in chapter 1, God set a precedent at Creation when He appeared the first time in the middle of darkness. He chose a mass of dark, chaotic, empty nothingness and hovered over it with His Holy Spirit. In the same manner, when it is time for us to come into a new chapter or era in our personal lives, there will always be an empty, unformed mass within us. The new thing needs to be brought to birth. That calls for a time of hovering and brooding and conceiving and forming on God's part.

Before God gets ready to create the new thing, He causes us to notice the darkness and the chaotic void so that we will begin to cry out to Him to come and do a new thing. He longs for us to invite Him to come. And this is the hardest part!

We Are in a Time of Hovering

A large deck connects to the back of my house. Under the deck are planks of cedar on which some birds have built two nests. Every spring when it is time to bring forth their new broods of chicks, the birds find those nests again. Every year, they lay their eggs in those nests. Then they sit on (hover over, brood over) those eggs until the new babies hatch. Following the hatching, the parents stay with those little, helpless chicks until they have grown enough to fend for themselves. So it is with God.

This is revelational. It gives meaning to that darkness that seems pointless and meaningless. It is dark because an internal seed in each of us is being planted in darkness for the purpose of germination. God comes and personally attends to that seed. When God is ready to transform something, He comes and lingers over it.

Some theologians believe the chaos in Genesis 1 resulted from the war in heaven when Lucifer turned against God. They say when Lucifer was thrown out of heaven to the earth, he ruined what God had originally created, and the chaos was the result. Whether this is the case or not, our Scripture begins with the first act of creation, in which God makes something out of nothing by hovering or lingering over the chaos.

He is still doing the same today. God is taking our nothingness, our personal emptiness, as well as the messes in our cities and nations, and He is hovering or brooding over them to form something new. By the precedent quite possibly set in Genesis, God chooses to come to *devastated* places to work His transformation. First, He often allows the devastation so that He can rebuild what has been ruined. Sometimes this devastation is called "judgment." God's judgment is redemptive—it brings down the old so that His new can be built.

Transforming the Darkness

God transforms the darkness over and over. It occurs all throughout Scripture. The Genesis account of Creation is the first example of when, by His hovering presence and stated will, light burst forth into the darkness.

Later, in Genesis 32, we see a transformation in Jacob, who could not go meet his brother, Esau, as long as he remained in his current state. First Jacob's nature, his very identity, needed to be transformed. Into the night an angel descended to wrestle with Jacob. Some theologians say it was God Himself rather than an angel who was wrestling with Jacob, a divine appearance that is called a *theophany*. All night, until daybreak, Jacob wrestled and struggled with the angel. In the darkness of that night, the angel broke Jacob's self-dependence.

During their encounter, Jacob grabbed hold of the angel and said, "I won't let you go until you bless me." At that point, he was still known as "Jacob," which means conniver or deceiver (the Amplified Bible adds supplanter, schemer, trickster and swindler). Once the angel got Jacob to admit his name, the angel then changed it to "Israel," which means "contender with God," and told him, "for you have contended and have power with God and with men and have prevailed" (Genesis 32:28, AMP). By wrestling through one long, dark night, Jacob was transformed.

Moving on to the book of Exodus, we read how Israel's deliverance took place in the night (see Exodus 12). In the account of the Passover, the angel of death passed over the people of Israel without taking any of Israel's firstborn. The Israelites were delivered from the death decree. But it was more than deliverance from death. If they had stayed in Egypt, the Israelites would have been exterminated as a people group. That night they slipped out of the hands of the Egyptians and took flight. In the middle of the night, they were delivered out of the hand of their masters. They were transformed from slaves in a foreign land to citizens of their own nation.

In Judges, it was at the midnight hour that Gideon entered into battle with the Midianites, under whose rule Israel had lived for seven years (see Judges 7). With his three hundred men, Gideon battled his way through to victory—in the middle of the night. God came into the midst of both the darkness of the nighttime and the dark intent of the enemy, using Gideon to overthrow the enemy army and free His people, Israel. Powerful things seem to happen in darkness.

The best scriptural example of God transforming the darkness took place at Jesus' cross. Because of the evil act of crucifying the Savior, the Bible tells us darkness enveloped the whole land from noon until 3:00 P.M. Through Jesus, God penetrated the darkness of evil and overthrew it once and for all. When Jesus cried out and said, "Father, into Your hands I commit My Spirit!" little did the enemy know that Jesus had just conquered death (Luke 23:46). Little did the enemy know that the next step would be the restoration of both life and light—life and light that could never again be killed, put out or extinguished.

Three days later, when the resurrection occurred, Satan knew. Jesus' death and resurrection forever changed the authority that Satan had possessed. Jesus' journey through darkness transformed the history of the world.

We find further examples as we read the rest of the New Testament. When Paul and Silas were thrown into prison, they sang to God in the darkest part of night. What a model— singing in prison at midnight! I believe their singing set in motion the power and presence of God, and a miracle began to unfold. An earthquake shook the foundation of the prison. The doors opened. Everyone's shackles were unfastened. Paul and Silas were freed. And the prison keeper became a follower of Jesus.

What would happen if you and I, like Paul and Silas, sang in our midnight hour? Darkness can become the invitation from God to do something new in our lives. Do not be intimidated by darkness. The darkness is our opportunity to enter a whole new place.

Cry Out

Sometimes it is hard to worship. It seems as if the darkness steals your breath away. But you can still call out to God. Even from the deepest pit you could be in, He will hear you. Remember, He is not afraid of the darkness.

I went to a church in the darkest part of Detroit, where I ministered to about thirty people. They brought along a number of children. All of a sudden, I saw this evil spirit on the children, smothering their spirits with darkness. I called the children forward so I could minister to them. When they came up, they started wailing. I had never seen anything like it.

These were kids who lived in the middle of the worst kind of urban darkness imaginable. They had experienced every kind of abuse. Every week they saw people shot or beaten up. Most of them knew people who had been violently murdered.

One little girl wailed so long and so loudly that I just picked her up like a mother to comfort her while I prayed. I held her for 45 minutes, speaking into her to break the power of the evil that had infiltrated her soul and spirit. Finally, she quieted down, and the spirit that controlled her left. She and the other children lived in a place gone horribly wrong, with people whose lives were chaotic, disordered and dangerous. But they did not live too far away for God to reach them. He heard their cries. He listened to their wailing. To His ears, their cries sounded just like prayers.

Leveled for the New

Your night experience, your dark night of the soul, is God's ticket for you to catch a ride to a whole new place in Him. Only as we walk through the night do we qualify to penetrate the darkness in a whole new way. By our successful passage through it, we gain a new authority over the dark night. Painful as it may be, nothing can replace the ability of the night to bring you and me through to a place of new identity, expanded power, increased influence, heightened authority and even, ultimately, honor.

Before God does something new with His people, He first prepares us by allowing us to go through a leveling experience in which our dependence on Him is birthed in a new way. In the darkness, you and I lose the positions we had in the past. Our sense of importance is leveled. But we come up out of that place leaning on God, dependent on Him in an all-new way.

Is that what is happening in your life right now? Are you being leveled? If you are, you are on track. God's bulldozer is clearing the way so that He can build something all new inside you.

3

The God Who Is Light

Several years ago, while on a ministry trip to a geographic location that seemed particularly "dark," I stumbled onto a new way of thinking. That thinking has since then reframed my whole approach to challenging circumstances.

Upon entering the airspace above that troubled region, I had already started feeling uncomfortable and ill at ease. I did not know why, but I knew enough to pay attention to that feeling. When I disembarked from the plane, the person who met me wasted no time before telling me how dreadful it was to live in that locale. What an unusual way to greet a guest!

I looked around as we drove to our destination. Though breathtakingly beautiful, the area seemed very poor. I saw many shabbily constructed, unkempt houses and failed businesses, even some deserted villages. Alcoholism and drug addiction were major social problems. Jobs were scarce, and poverty abounded.

Hopelessness slapped me in the face like flapjacks on a griddle. I would look at the landscape, and its beauty would take my breath away. Then I would look at the people and the places they lived, and the life would drain back out of me. The pervading spiritual, mental and emotional darkness made everything bleak. The sense of despair pulled me down. "Poverty" and "lack" were written across the empty, emotionless faces of the residents. They seemed deficient in something.

In just about every way, the people in this region were impoverished—financially, spiritually, emotionally and relationally. Their poverty was a type of darkness. It was depressing because it was the opposite of what God is like.

God is never depressed. His Kingdom is not characterized by poverty. He is the God who lifts heavy burdens. He is the God who loves us. He reverses the work of the enemy. He is light, and He is life. "In Him was life, and the life was the light of men" (John 1:4). He is "the Bright and Morning Star" (Revelation 22:16). He is the God who is wisdom, redemption, sanctification, restoration, cleansing and healing.

Jesus came to show us the way out of our darkness. Look at the words of Zachariah's prophecy over his son, John the Baptist:

> And you, my child, "Prophet of the Highest," will go ahead of the Master to prepare his ways, present the offer of salvation to his people, the forgiveness of their sins. Through the heartfelt mercies of our God, God's Sunrise will break in upon us, shining on those in the darkness, those sitting in the shadow of death, then showing us the way, one foot at a time, down the path of peace.
>
> Luke 1:76–79, MESSAGE

Now I had been called as a light in the midst of that dark region, a representative of the Kingdom of Light. I had been summoned to minister here. What could I offer them? I found myself crying out inside, *Oh God, what about this? What am I to say? What am I to do? What answers do I have?*

Arriving at the hotel, I spent some time in prayer. I began to get in touch with God's heart, and He began to impress my heart with a specific Scripture verse. It was not one of my top ten verses, nor had it ever stood out to me before. How could Genesis 1, verse 2 help me minister to these people? Why did God whisper that Scripture to me? I felt sure it must hold a key, so I read it over and over: "The earth was without form, and void; and darkness was on the face of the deep. And the Spirit of God was hovering over the face of the waters."

It certainly seemed like an unusual place to start, but as I pulled up the passage on my laptop's Bible software, lightbulbs began to light up in my heart and mind. My despair and hopelessness over this assignment began to dissipate as the reality of one application of this verse dawned on me.

As I read it, I began to realize that no person, no situation and no physical region is ever beyond God's ability to change things. Nothing we could ever face, including the most extreme disaster imaginable, could ever be a bigger job for God than was the Creation. And the One who brought order into that chaotic emptiness and light into that utter darkness could of course do the same in lesser situations. Moreover, I saw that He *wants* to bring His light into the darkness. He stands ready to do it.

I also saw that in order for God to transform the darkness into light, His Holy Spirit needs to hover over it as He hovered over the darkness at the Creation. He needs to linger over our darkness, staying as close as a brooding mother bird. When the Holy Spirit shows up and begins to hover and to linger, you and I must realize something great is about to happen!

ls to Transformation

n to sense that the Holy Spirit is "brooding
he deep" in your situation, you need to wel-
‑‑‑‑ hovering presence. And you need to recognize
that, although the process may take some time, He will not
remain in hovering mode forever. His work is time sensitive.
Be ready to move with Him when it is time to "hatch" a new
thing, and cooperate with Him during the ensuing process
of nurturing it.

I remember the care my mother gave me when I was sick
as a child. She would hover over me and stay close until I was
well again. She would cover me up, fix special food for me,
hold me when I needed it, stroke my head, fix my bed and ask
me how I was doing. Was I getting better? Feeling worse? Her
primary motherly concern was to bring me back to bright-
eyed health.

When my father came home from work, he would hide my
pills in a piece of a Peppermint Pattie so I would take them.
He knew that I would gag and choke if given a pill by itself.
He would rub my back, talk to me and sometimes read me
stories. He, too, hovered over me because he wanted to see
me restored to health.

What I came to understand that day in my hotel room
in that dark locale grew into a dynamic conviction that no
darkness, no confusion, no problem has the final word. The
Bible begins in Genesis with God entering a chaotic earth
to finish the creative process. Some theologians teach that
everything that happens in the Bible is found in Genesis in
seed form. That idea formed a foundational understanding
for me that to this day frames the way I approach a chaotic
situation. God longs to come and hover over our darkness,
over our chaos (personal or societal) and transform it. He
will transform our darkness into light. Though this is not

theologically "correct," it is as if He is attracted to our darkness to transform it.

God, who is Life and Light, has the final word.

You can depend on it: When you sense God hovering over you or your family, your church or your city, you can know that He is preparing to creatively transform something, to bring light into the darkness. That revelation alone should be enough to lighten your darkness!

First God hovers, then He creates. When He begins to hover, that is *not* the time for you to busy yourself thinking about structure and form. That will come later. It is the time to nurture His presence, to wait upon Him. It is the time to welcome His presence, to cherish His presence, to guard over and to protect your openness to His presence. It is the time to let your hope replace despair, not the time to think up new methods or try to reorganize anything.

At the Creation, the Holy Spirit came and brooded over the void. He did not sit in judgment to condemn or destroy; He hovered in a deliberate manner for the purpose of bringing forth a newly created order of life. So it is with us. A period of incubation, waiting and warming, always precedes the moment when the new is conceived and formed, nurtured and matured.

When God begins to hover, your response should be to wait upon Him. Spend time with Him. Turn your face toward His light. Soak it up. Trust Him. He has come to save you.

Totally focus on waiting upon the Lord. If you will do that, you will find yourself in a welcome new place. It will refresh, revive and resurrect you. If you get busy and try to "help" God, you may have to start over. This was the difference between Mary and Martha. Mary simply came into Jesus' presence and waited, listening to His words. Martha busied herself with work. Martha's work itself was not wrong, but her timing was off. There is both a time to work and a time to wait, but this was not a time for "doing" in God's presence—it was a time for simply "being" in God's presence.

Job understood the necessity of waiting. He said, "All the days of my hard service I will *wait*, till my *change* comes" (Job 14:14, emphasis added). In Job's darkest hour, God was hovering over him, bringing forth something new.

> Therefore the LORD will wait, that He may be gracious
>   to you;
> And therefore He will be exalted, that He may have
>   mercy on you.
> For the LORD is a God of justice;
> Blessed are all those who wait for Him.
>
> Isaiah 30:18

God's renewing power is released in the waiting. He does not leave anything half-done. Not only will renewal come to those who wait for God's timing, but also they will learn to *fly*. Transformed, they will be able to catch the updrafts and soar freely with God's presence and purpose. They will run without any weariness and walk without fainting, because they waited while the Lord hovered over them. They waited until He created something new inside them so that they could go forth in His strength and power rather than their own. Remember how Isaiah put it: "Those who wait on the LORD shall renew their strength; they shall mount up with wings like eagles, they shall run and not be weary, they shall walk and not faint" (Isaiah 40:31).

Darkness Does Not Intimidate God

God is with us from start to finish throughout this process of transformation. Darkness and light are both alike to Him. He is not afraid of the dark because He Himself is Light. God not only refuses to let darkness intimidate Him, He *dwells* in it:

He bowed the heavens also and came down; and thick darkness
was under His feet. And He rode upon a cherub [a storm] and
flew [swiftly]; yes, He sped on with the wings of the wind. He
made darkness His secret hiding place; as His pavilion (His
canopy) round about Him were dark waters and thick clouds
of the skies.

Psalm 18:9–11, AMP

By dwelling in our darkness, God dispatches it. He sends it
away. He floods it with light. He achieves what would otherwise be impossible:

> The waves of death swirled about me;
>   the torrents of destruction overwhelmed me.
> The cords of the grave coiled around me;
>   the snares of death confronted me.
> In my distress I called to the LORD;
>   I called out to my God.
> From his temple he heard my voice;
>   my cry came to his ears.
> The earth trembled and quaked,
>   the foundations of the heavens shook;
>   they trembled because he was angry. . . .
> He parted the heavens and came down;
>   dark clouds were under his feet.
> He mounted the cherubim and flew;
>   he soared on the wings of the wind.
> He made darkness his canopy around him—
>   the dark rain clouds of the sky.
> Out of the brightness of his presence
>   bolts of lightning blazed forth.
> The LORD thundered from heaven;
>   the voice of the Most High resounded.
> He shot arrows and scattered the enemies,
>   bolts of lightning and routed them. . . .
> He reached down from on high and took hold of me;
>   he drew me out of deep waters.

He rescued me from my powerful enemy,
   from my foes, who were too strong for me.
They confronted me in the day of my disaster,
   but the LORD was my support.
He brought me out into a spacious place;
   he rescued me because he delighted in me. . . .
You are my lamp, O LORD;
   the LORD turns my darkness into light.

2 Samuel 22:5–8, 10–15, 17–20, 29, NIV

In essence, our whole life as believers in Jesus Christ is a battle between light and darkness. That battle is both internal and personal, and external, relating to the world we live in. There are two kingdoms in the universe, the Kingdom of Light, or God's, and the kingdom of darkness, or Satan's. Jesus came as the Light of the world. His assignment was to overcome Satan's power, or the power of darkness, so that you and I could come into our original destiny as the offspring of God, possessing His nature and restorative passion. He has delivered us from the control and dominion of darkness: "[The Father] has delivered and drawn us to Himself out of the control and the dominion of darkness and has transferred us into the kingdom of the Son of His love" (Colossians 1:13, AMP).

Worship the God Who Is Light

With such a God as ours, the Lord over our darkness, we go down on our knees in worship. Without hesitation, we accept His assignment to us, which is to represent Him by becoming lights in the midst of the darkness around us.

For you were once darkness, but now you are light in the Lord. Walk as children of light (for the fruit of the Spirit is in all goodness, righteousness, and truth), finding out what is acceptable to the Lord. And have no fellowship with the unfruitful works of darkness, but rather expose them. For it is shameful even to speak of those things which are done by them in secret. But all things that are exposed are made manifest by the light, for whatever makes manifest is light. Therefore He says: "Awake, you who sleep, arise from the dead, and Christ will give you light."

Ephesians 5:8–14

Our darkness resulted because we bowed down to another will, even if we did not know what we were doing. Now that the Lord has come to alleviate our darkness, we can align our will to God's will and gratefully, trustfully worship Him.

Who else but our God could have done this thing? He loves us so much that He continually takes the initiative in our lives to reach into our darkness—even though most often our darkness represents a violation of His will—to show us the path toward single-hearted devotion. He does not want us subject to the devil any longer, on any level.

When Lucifer sinned by rebelling against God in heaven before any of us were created, he split his will from God's on purpose. He wanted to receive worship himself. He did not want to give all of his worship to God. He was thrown down from heaven as a result, taking with him other angels who now make up the hosts of hell. In his desire to dominate and spoil more of God's universe, he has tirelessly worked to undermine the progress of God's Kingdom and to introduce as much darkness as possible. Ever since Satan introduced sin into the human race, we, too, struggle with "two wills," our own (reinforced by Satan's), and God's.

But our God is not only Light, He is Love. He hears our cries. He comes. He hovers. He does whatever is necessary to turn our faces back to His. He closes the distance. He conquers the void.

The story of Joe Eszterhas illustrates what I mean. Joe is an author. He was the screenwriter for the movie *Basic Instinct*. In 2001, at the age of fifty-six, he was diagnosed with throat cancer. Doctors removed 80 percent of his larynx, inserted a tracheotomy tube in his throat and advised him to stop drinking and smoking immediately. An article by David Yonke of the *Toledo Blade* later described Eszterhas's battle for life and health:

> At age 56, after a lifetime of wild living, Mr. Eszterhas knew it would be a struggle to change his ways.
>
> One hot summer day after his surgery, walking through his tree-lined neighborhood, . . . Mr. Eszterhas reached a breaking point.
>
> "I was going crazy. I was jittery. I twitched. I trembled. I had no patience for anything. Every single nerve ending was demanding a drink and a cigarette," he wrote.
>
> He plopped down on a curb and cried. Sobbed, even. And for the first time since he was a child, he prayed, "Please God, help me."
>
> Mr. Eszterhas was shocked by his own prayer.
>
> "I couldn't believe I'd said it. I didn't know why I'd said it. I'd never said it before," he wrote.
>
> But he felt an overwhelming peace. His heart stopped pounding. His hands stopped twitching. He saw a "shimmer, dazzling, nearly blinding brightness that made me cover my eyes with my hands."
>
> Like Saul on the road to Damascus, Mr. Eszterhas had been blinded by God. He stood up, wiped his eyes, and walked back home a new man.[1]

Before his illness, Eszterhas wrote script after script for movies with dark themes and sinister plots. Sixteen of his dark-centered scripts made it to the big screen—some paying as much as $3 million a script. But after his spiritual transformation, he decided he had spent far too much of his life concentrating on the dark side. He decided he had had enough of murder, blood and chaos. He decided he was ready to come out of the darkness into the light. In the article, he explained his change this way:

> Frankly, my life changed from the moment God entered my heart. I'm not interested in darkness anymore. I've got four gorgeous boys, a wife I adore, I love being alive, and I love and enjoy every moment of my life. My view has brightened and I don't want to go back into that dark place.[2]

The article goes on to say that Eszterhas's love and appreciation for life was magnified even more in 2007 when he received a report from his surgeon that his throat cancer had been cured. Although oncologists rarely use the word *cured*, he was told he did not need to return for checkups because his throat tissue had regenerated to the point where the doctor could no longer tell that he had had cancer. Not only that, but there was no remaining evidence of surgery. The Light of Jesus had brought new life *and* miraculous healing.

Speaking the Word into the Darkness

When the Light comes into our darkness, our waiting time becomes a growing time. To "keep the lights on," what better nourishment for new life than the Word, Christ Himself? Just as important as the creative word of God, the prophetic word, is the foundational truth we can obtain from the Scriptures and from the Holy Spirit's still, small voice in our hearts. Paul exhorted his son in the faith, Timothy, to study the Word and be diligent in his walk with God (see 2 Timothy 2:15).

Jesus Christ came to us as the Light of the world. He lightens our darkness by opening our blind eyes and freeing us from the places where darkness has imprisoned us. His nature is filled with light. Revelation causes the light of God to overthrow darkness. No wonder we say "the lights came on" when we speak of a revelation. Once the light comes on, we can see what to do.

Years ago, I was praying for my cousin who had brain cancer. In prayer, I saw a detailed vision of demonic figures who were holding his cancer in place. Having seen these evil powers, I could do something about them. I prayed until I saw every one of them broken and removed. Within a short period of time after I finished praying, I received the news that my cousin was cancer free. With God's light shining on the situation, I could see what to do and could hold on in prayer until God's will had been accomplished.

With God, there is no darkness or shadow of turning, says James 1:17. Here's how the MESSAGE translation renders that passage:

> So, my very dear friends, don't get thrown off course. Every desirable and beneficial gift comes out of heaven. The gifts are rivers of light cascading down from the Father of Light. There is nothing deceitful in God, nothing two-faced, nothing fickle. He brought us to life using the true Word, showing us off as the crown of all his creatures.
>
> James 1:16–18

Once we connect with God, the lights go on. Then with Isaiah, we can shout:

> Arise, shine;
> For your light has come!
> And the glory of the LORD is risen upon you.
> For behold, the darkness shall cover the earth,
> And deep darkness the people;

But the LORD will arise over you,
And His glory will be seen upon you.
The Gentiles shall come to your light,
And kings to the brightness of your rising.

Isaiah 60:1–3

4

The Breaking of the New Day

We use the term "dark night of the soul" often, usually without realizing where it comes from. It was the title of a book by a sixteenth-century Spanish priest known as St. John of the Cross, and it has been used widely to describe a time of deep spiritual distress that turns out to be productive for an individual in the long run. In the long "night" a person is transformed, especially in his or her relationship with God.

Here is a sample from St. John of the Cross's second volume of *Dark Night of the Soul*:

> Even though this blessed night darkens the spirit, it does so only to impart light in all things. And even though it humbles us and reveals our miseries, it does so only to exalt us. And even though it impoverishes us and empties us of all our possessions and natural affections, it does so only that we may reach

forward divinely to the enjoyment of everything in heaven and on earth, all the while preserving a general freedom of spirit in them all.[1]

The "dark night of the soul" is one of the terms I use in *The Overcomer's Anointing* to describe our personal experience of darkness. Even when you would not use "dark night of the soul" to describe what you are going through, your "night" will share certain important characteristics with the mental, emotional and spiritual wasteland that St. John of the Cross described. At the least, you can expect that your night will be divided into identifiable stages, which we sometimes call "watches of the night."

The ancient Jews did not have wristwatches or clocks to tell time by, especially in the middle of the night. They divided the night into military "watches" that consisted of three hours at a stretch. Throughout the New Testament, they would tell time by identifying what watch it was. We find "the fourth watch of the night," for instance, in the story of Jesus walking on the water in Matthew 14:25 and Mark 6:48.

In the gospels, the four watches are known as evening (6:00 to 9:00 P.M.), midnight (9:00 P.M. to midnight), cock-crowing (midnight to 3:00 A.M.) and morning (3:00 to 6:00 A.M.). Mark 13:35 is one verse that identifies them: "Watch therefore, for you do not know when the master of the house is coming—in the evening, at midnight, at the crowing of the rooster, or in the morning."

Keeping these night watches in mind, let's look more closely at the typical stages or phases of a dark night of the soul.

Pressing through the Dark Night of the Soul

For a long time, even for years, prophets have been telling us that we are entering a "new day." Some people have gotten so tired of hearing that phrase that they have tuned it out. The reality in which you and I live can seem very distant from a new day. In fact, rather than the breaking of a new day, it sometimes feels like the breaking *down* of any possibility of ever welcoming a new day. So often it seems as if the life we once enjoyed has withered away—as if our dreams, hopes and visions have disappeared. As the darkness and strife in the world around us has intensified, the darkness within our souls has deepened.

Descent into Darkness

In Genesis 1, did you ever notice that the new day started in the evening? In other words, *the first part of the new day involved increasing darkness.*

At the completion of God's first creative act, the narrator wrote: "So the evening and the morning were the first day" (Genesis 1:5). After each successive day, that statement is repeated. Biblically, a new day commences just as it begins to get dark. This is true in every application. Your new day also begins with a descent into darkness.

We never seem to expect it. When a new prophetic word from God comes, enough light remains so that we rejoice, dance, shout and tell everyone about our great news—totally unsuspecting that we are about to be thrust into deep darkness. The new day has arrived! The light has dawned! Then the light begins to fade. What is happening?

We have simply misinterpreted the situation. Most of us think that the darkness of night indicates the end of the old day—not the beginning of the next one. But what sometimes appears as the end is really a new beginning. As the lights go out on the previous day, the degree of available light deteriorates until we find ourselves in pitch blackness around midnight, the darkest part of the new day. From then on, we notice a gradual emergence of increasing light, which climaxes with dawn, the "breaking" of day. Did the day begin at dawn? No—according to God's timetable, the new day has been unfolding for hours. At 6:00 A.M., we can finally see what started at 6:00 P.M. the previous evening, as darkness fell.

What Happens in the Night?

Several things happen during the hours of darkness. First, nighttime is intended as a time of rest, refreshment and renewal for the new day. It is a time to regroup and get ready to meet the new day's challenges. At the beginning of your new day, God announces to you what He is going to do. He visits you and declares what your call and position will be in this new day. In the evening, you gather your faculties to envision and prepare for it.

Consider how Isaac took time to meditate in the evening. That is when he saw his provision for the future. He saw camels coming, and camels represent provision.[2] "And Isaac went out to meditate in the field in the evening; and he lifted his eyes and looked, and there, the camels were coming" (Genesis 24:63).

Isaac positioned himself to move into his future. If we, too, will take time to meditate on God, as well as on His Word and promises, oftentimes in the evening He will give us glimpses of His provision for our future. I have found that He will even speak to me in dreams while I sleep.

The nighttime is also our opportunity to overcome our fear of darkness. God will make sure we are ready for the fulfillment of His call to us. He will make sure we are not just stumbling through the dark. We would do well to pay attention to God in the quiet hours of the evening.

> We have the prophetic word [made] firmer still. You will do well to pay close attention to it as to a lamp shining in a dismal (squalid and dark) place, until the day breaks through

[the gloom] and the Morning Star rises (comes into being) in your hearts.

2 Peter 1:19, AMP

Next Comes War

As we pass through the evening into the darkness of night, we are walking through a new "gate." We step over the threshold, through the narrow opening, into the new place. And, whether we want it or not, we will always find war at the gate to the new.[3]

After a period of elation about a new call from God, our excitement subsides with the onset of darkness and trials. Like Joseph, we go through a time of testing. Once we felt like favored dreamers, but now we find ourselves in a dark prison.

These trials prepare us for the fulfillment of the call. God pronounced the biblical precedent for inheritance in the book of Revelation. God declared to each of the churches that if they would overcome in their particular test, they would inherit something.

Furthermore, God wants to make sure we arrive at the new place having turned out the lights to the previous day. We seldom understand what He is doing. How can this darkness be good? It is getting darker and darker. We struggle to believe and to follow Him. We keep trying to turn the lights back on. We feel disconnected, disoriented and alone, so sometimes we try to go back where we were before. But such feelings come with the path we are on to a new day. Let's look for a minute at why.

Disconnection: A disconnection must take place if we are to make our way into the new. It may be a disconnection with old ideas, beliefs and emotions. It may mean accepting a new role and a subsequent reordering of relationships. It may involve detaching or disentangling ourselves from dysfunctional aspects of relationships. Just as Joseph was physically removed from his homeland, so we must be removed either physically or psychologically.

Jonathan was unable to disconnect emotionally from his father, Saul. As a result, Jonathan never saw the new day. But David did. Orpah was unwilling to emotionally disconnect from her people in Moab, but Ruth was willing. So Ruth alone followed Naomi to Bethlehem, the place of visitation and inheritance. Because Ruth was willing to disconnect from her past, she was the one who stepped into the new day.

Disorientation and aloneness: With disconnection comes disorientation. You no longer have a firm grip on who you are or where you are. You may come to the place where you feel as if you are barely hanging on, and that may make you fight even harder because you do not understand what is happening. How do you hang on when nothing is left to hold on to? You frantically grab anything, trying with all your might to hang on lest you lose your grip and fall.

It is dark, and you feel very alone. It can be frightening. Stranded in a place where nothing is working and nobody seems to understand, the old glory has departed; only hollowness remains. Your joy and motivation are gone. You do not really want to go back where you came from, but you have no idea yet where to go next. That is why we cry out at times, like the Israelites, "Just let us go back to the leeks and the garlic!" We think, *Let me return to something I felt comfortable with, someplace I can call "home."* Like the psalmist, you and I can feel overwhelmed:

> In the day of my trouble I sought the Lord;
> My hand was stretched out in the night without
>   ceasing;

My soul refused to be comforted.
I remembered God, and was troubled;
I complained, and my spirit was overwhelmed.   Selah

You hold my eyelids open;
I am so troubled that I cannot speak.
I have considered the days of old,
The years of ancient times.
I call to remembrance my song in the night;
I meditate within my heart,
And my spirit makes diligent search.

Will the Lord cast off forever?
And will He be favorable no more?
Has His mercy ceased forever?
Has His promise failed forevermore?
Has God forgotten to be gracious?
Has He in anger shut up His tender mercies?   Selah

Psalm 77:2–9

Because you and I do not understand what is happening, we struggle and battle for our "rights." My dog, Missy, does this all the time. When I bring her fresh food, old food often still remains in her bowl. Rather than allowing me to remove the old food so that I can replace it with the new, she will growl and fight for the little scraps she has left. She does not understand that something new and better is about to arrive.

This difficult stretch of time is like the biblical second watch, the midnight watch. In his book *God's Unfolding Battle Plan*, Chuck Pierce, a world-renowned prophetic voice and strategist, comments,

The midnight watch begins at 9:00 P.M. and goes to the middle of the night. The word "midnight" is often used symbolically of a time period of intense darkness or extended gloom. Many times we try to sleep during this hour, yet sleep escapes us because of our anxiety.

This is also the time when God deals with our enemies that are trying to keep us from entering into His perfect plan for our lives. It was at midnight that the Lord struck down all the firstborn in the land of Egypt (see Exodus 11:4; 12:29).

In essence, midnight is a defining point.[4]

The Midnight Hour

Then comes the actual midnight hour. It is the pivotal point. The midnight hour is the time of greatest intensity, the hour when darkness can be *felt*. It can be likened to Jesus crying out on the cross, "My God, My God, why have You forsaken Me?" (Matthew 27:46).

In order for something new to replace it, the old must be put to death. The midnight hour is when death comes. The final blow is dealt to the past. There is nothing more you can do. The fight is over—you have no fight left in you. You feel as though there is nowhere to turn, no one to help you, nothing left to do—you have tried it all. You have been totally emptied. You have exhausted every option except surrender.

You may feel like Job did when he said,

> I go to the place from which I shall not return,
> To the land of darkness and the shadow of death,
> A land as dark as darkness itself,
> As the shadow of death, without any order,
> Where even the light is like darkness.
>
> Job 10:21–22

This is the ultimate trial of your faith. Will you continue to believe the word of the Lord to you in spite of death? The midnight hour brings death to your vision, your ministry, your level of anointing, your relationships, so that the greater good, the new day, can break forth. Will you trust God enough to press through until the dawn?

Peter denied Christ in the middle of the night. Yet he came through this temporary defeat to a place of great victory. His failure did not mark the end of the story. Later in his life, he wrote:

> [You should] be exceedingly glad on this account, though now for a little while you may be distressed by trials and suffer temptations, so that [the genuineness] of your faith may be tested, [your faith] which is infinitely more precious than the perishable gold which is tested and purified by fire. [This proving of your faith is intended] to redound to [your] praise and glory and honor when Jesus Christ (the Messiah, the Anointed one) is revealed. Without having seen Him, you love Him; though you do not [even] now see Him, you believe in Him and exult and thrill with inexpressible and glorious (triumphant, heavenly) joy. [At the same time] you receive the result (outcome, consummation) of your faith, the salvation of your souls.
>
> 1 Peter 1:6–9, AMP

> Beloved, do not be amazed and bewildered at the fiery ordeal which is taking place to test your quality, as though something strange (unusual and alien to you and your position) were befalling you. But insofar as you are sharing Christ's sufferings, rejoice, so that when His glory [full of radiance and splendor] is revealed, you may also rejoice with triumph [exultantly].
>
> 1 Peter 4:12–13, AMP

In his book *Critical Mass*, in a chapter called "The Dark Night of the Soul," Bible teacher Mario Murillo wrote:

> [There is a] key similarity between revival and nuclear fission, ... a strange phenomenon that occurs right before the atom

splits. The nucleus actually depresses. Scientists observe that the neutron bombardment which seemed to be changing the nucleus, now shows no sign of reaching critical mass. Nothing seems to be happening.

That is also what happens right before a manifestation of God's glory. The revival core will be praying and sensing a rising tide of power and expectancy. All of a sudden, you hit a brick wall. The power is gone. God's presence seems to have lifted. Your prayers feel trapped in your mouth. A deep despair settles in. You feel physically drained.

This is the dark night of the soul. This is where every revival pioneer has been before you and now it's your turn. It will take everything in you to keep moving. The sobering fact is that many who have reached the dark night of the soul have retreated. Eternity will reveal a long, sad history of revival near-misses. . . .

At no other time does God express love more than when He allows this time of total emptiness. God risks being misunderstood. He faces the potential of one of His children walking away frustrated and confused, but He believes the good it will produce is well worth the risk.[5]

The midnight hour is the ultimate test.

The Death Process

Before He entered the death process, Jesus said, "Unless a grain of wheat falls into the ground and dies, it remains alone; but if it dies, it produces much grain" (John 12:24). Now, in the midnight hour, death comes to our ability to succeed, to our arrogant striving to produce something, to our mental strength and to our ability to work things out. You and I must come to that place of total helplessness where we completely surrender ourselves to God. We need to let go of our reputation, place, position, relationships—everything. Furthermore, we need to come to a place of peace within our total helplessness where we put *all* of our trust in God's hands.

At midnight, you and I stumble onto the spiritual experience of Galatians 2:20: "I have been crucified with Christ; it is no longer I who live, but Christ lives in me; and the life which I now live in the flesh I live by faith in the Son of God, who loved me and gave Himself for me."

Our ego—our trust in ourselves and in our human capabilities—is now gone. It has been exhausted, emptied. Like Jesus, we say, "Without God, I can do nothing" (see John 5:30). Like Jesus, we place the will of God above our own will. We die to our own will and choose His.

This can be more difficult for some than for others. In America, for example, I think our culture has become self-focused and self-centered. We do not talk very much about "dying to ourselves." In fact, we feel very protective of our self-esteem, which we think we will lose in the process. We Americans are not very good at giving away our lives. We are not very altruistic; we do not care more about others than we do about ourselves. We are not very good at persevering through hardship, probably because we have been brought up in a world of instant everything. The loudest messages many of us hear are about achieving success at the expense of others. We are expected to strive to accrue wealth and fame, not to find ways to die to ourselves.

So it seems strange to many of us when someone gives up the rights to his or her life in order to pastor a church and give away life to other people. It seems unusual for a person to willingly accept being inconvenienced or put down or persecuted. But dying to self is the way it works in the Kingdom of God.

Before He talked about the grain of wheat dying, Jesus said that the time had come for the Son of Man to be glorified. You and I love glory. We love to be well thought of and admired. It is tempting to take that kind of glory. But what kind of glory was Jesus referring to? The road to true glory led Jesus through

Gethsemane and then Calvary, all the way to death on the cross.

Your road to glory in God's Kingdom will take you down a similar path, a dying to self to magnify God's will and plans above your own. Your dying to self will reflect the stages a person goes through when dying a physical death. In a midnight hour, you will face the finality of your situation. This is it! You cannot return to your youth or health or whatever it is you are giving up. You will go through confusion and disillusionment. You will not feel as if you are doing anything right. Maybe you are not confessing enough or praying enough or whatever. Eventually, you will give up your idealistic notions, your illusions.

Still, you will not be sure that this death process is worth anything. You will try alternative processes. If you always achieved victory in the past by reading certain Scripture passages, you will try that. If it helped to listen to worship music, you will try that. Anything to end the pain.

Eventually, you will find there is no place to run to anymore. Emotionally, you will feel raw, anxious, irritated, fearful. You cannot run away from yourself. You cannot hide from yourself. But if you lay down your rights to have your life turn out in a certain preconceived way, you will gain something better. The degree of your death to self indicates the degree of transformation that you can expect to experience.

If you go all the way down to the bottom of your heart, you will find your doubt. You will find the places where your will is counter to God's will. You will encounter both your fear and your faith. And then you can truly lay it all down and prepare for the coming new day.

Sweet Surrender

What freedom you find in finally letting go of all striving and anxiety over the future! In the dark night of your soul, you come to understand that there is no way to release your future except through obedience. You no longer carry your life on your shoulders. No longer does your future depend on you; it rests on God.

The night is over; its work is finished; it has transformed your heart and mind. Released into a new place with God, a place of total trust, reliance and faith in Him, you no longer call your faith "my" faith; it is now God's faith released within you. You have just moved from who you are in Christ, to who Christ is in you.

You have just found out what it is to be a true human being. The paradox of it all—dying to be made fully alive! Finding newness through brokenness! When did the precious ointment in the alabaster box become life-giving? When the box was broken (see Matthew 26:6–12).

Finally, you have overcome your fear of the night and the darkness, and you have broken through to a new faith and trust. You have just emerged from a death process, the death of yourself.

The Dawn—Releasing God's Glory

After God announces the promise of a new day in our lives, we press through the watches of the long night. Holding on to His promise in faith, we move into the most difficult time, when the vision seems to disappear in the darkening gloom. However, finally the midnight hour passes, the work is over and the sun rises to announce the new day. The MESSAGE Bible puts it this way:

> Forget about what's happened;
>   don't keep going over old history.
> Be alert, be present. I'm about to do something brand-
>   new.
> It's bursting out! Don't you see it?

> There it is! I'm making a road through the desert,
> rivers in the badlands.

Isaiah 43:18–19, MESSAGE

God does the work in our hearts and minds, transforming us. Our job is to allow Him to work. When the new thing springs forth, our eyes are open and we see it. Now we can move with it. What a glorious place to arrive at. Finally, we breathe a sigh of relief. We see what has been happening, and we now understand.

The night has been arduous. At times it felt as if we were hanging on by the merest of threads. Somehow in the midst of the process, God finished preparing us to move into the new day. Can you thank Him that He loves you and me enough to let us struggle, even to get hurt, in order to ensure that we are fully prepared for our destiny?

He seemed to forsake us, but only for a short while so that He could complete an eternal work of glory in our hearts and minds. Now we will be fully ready and prepared for the new:

> "Sing, O barren woman,
>   you who never bore a child;
> burst into song, shout for joy,
>   you who were never in labor;
> because more are the children of the desolate woman
>   than of her who has a husband,"
>   says the LORD.
> "Enlarge the place of your tent,
>   stretch your tent curtains wide,
>   do not hold back;
> lengthen your cords,
>   strengthen your stakes.
> For you will spread out to the right and to the left;
>   your descendants will dispossess nations
>   and settle in their desolate cities."

Isaiah 54:1–3, NIV

Look at the old hymn "Watchman, Tell Us of the Night," which is a poetic interpretation of Isaiah 21:11–12. From evening to midnight to the glorious breaking of the dawn, our own experience echoes through its words:

Watchman, Tell Us of the Night

Watchman, tell us of the night,
What its signs of promise are.
Traveler, o'er yon mountain's height,
See that glory-beaming star!
Watchman, doth its beauteous ray
Aught of hope or joy foretell?
Traveler, yes—it brings the day,
Promised day of Israel.

Watchman, tell us of the night;
Higher yet that star ascends.
Traveler, blessedness and light,
Peace and truth, its course portends.
Watchman, will its beams alone
Gild the spot that gave them birth?
Traveler, ages are its own,
And it bursts o'er all the earth.

Watchman, tell us of the night,
For the morning seems to dawn.
Traveler, darkness takes its flight,
Doubt and terror are withdrawn.
Watchman, let thy wanderings cease;
Hie thee to thy quiet home.
Traveler, lo! the Prince of Peace,
Lo! the Son of God is come![6]

5

God's Heart for Restoration

When I was in my first year of college, my mother died. The dorm director, Mrs. Nordstrom, was responsible for informing me. That cold February day, I received the phone call to come to her apartment. Not knowing why I was summoned, I scooted down to her place. Within minutes I left numb, crushed, devastated, gasping for air, wondering if I would even live. And that was only the beginning. Within three weeks, I was back in her apartment. This time, she had to tell me that both my grandparents had died. Running out of her apartment, I was screaming, "How much can one person take?"

As far as I was concerned, my life was over. Everything within me died that winter. It took me several years to recover. It was too much to handle at such a young age. I had nothing on which to rest my experience of loss, and I did not know God in much depth. Consequently, I ended up an atheist for a season, then an agnostic. I blamed it all on God. Not only did I blame it on God, but I also blamed it on people—I blamed everybody for something. I was overtaken with anger, striking out at anyone about anything.

Though externally I went on, internally I had shut down, quit. I had resigned from faith, from optimism and from believing in God. Getting up every morning was an act of sheer bravery; usually it was the last thing I wanted to do. At times I felt I never would see the light of day again.

Ultimately, my misery forced me to find the genuine God in an authentic way. I did get there. Not only did God retrieve His lost, wandering, angry and confused vagabond, but He began a process of restoration in me that, although not instantaneous, was more than enough. He restored my soul. He brought me out into a wide place (see Psalm 18:16–19). He proved Himself faithful, and for the rest of my days I am proclaiming both His goodness and His greatness.

Not Such a Good Life

Chuck Colson had just finished writing a book called *The Good Life* when he was plunged into a very dark night. In an article for *Christianity Today*, he said about that time:

> What happens in the dark night of the soul? I found out this past year [2005]. Weeks after finishing *The Good Life*, my son Wendell was diagnosed with bone cancer. The operation to remove a malignant tumor took 10 hours—the longest day of my life. Wendell survived, but he's still in chemo.
>
> I had barely caught my breath when my daughter, Emily, was diagnosed with melanoma.
>
> Back in the hospital, I again prayed fervently. Soon after, my wife, Patty, underwent major knee surgery. Where was my good life?[1]

Exhausted from hospitals, two years of writing *The Good Life* and other challenging situations in his life, Colson said he was at his weakest when he found himself wrestling with the prince of darkness. He walked around asking God why He would allow all this, and he longed for the closeness with God he had experienced even in the darkest days of his prison term.

Yet Colson also thought about something the great evangelist Charles Spurgeon once wrote: "When thy God hides his face, say not that he has forgotten thee. He is but tarrying a little while to make thee love him better, and when he cometh, thou shalt have joy in the Lord and shalt rejoice with joy unspeakable." Colson commented that our evangelical forebears traditionally suggested that "faith becomes strongest when we are without consolation and must walk into the darkness with complete abandon." With that in mind, he went on to make an important statement about faith:

> It struck me that I don't have to make sense of the agonies I bear or hear a clear answer. God is not a creature of my emotions or senses. God is God, the one who created me and takes responsibility for my children's destiny and mine. I can only cling to the certainty that he is and he has spoken. . . .
>
> Faith isn't really faith if we can always rely on the still, small voice of God cheering us on. A prominent pastor once told me he experienced the Holy Spirit's presence every moment. Contemporary evangelicals regard this as maturity. Perhaps it is—or maybe it is a form of presumption. *True faith trusts even when every outward reality tells us there is no reason to.*[2]

God, the Restorer of Lost Inheritance

Throughout Scripture, God reveals Himself not just as the Creator, but also as the Redeemer, the Reconciler and the

Restorer. Although the term is not used as such, God the Restorer is found again and again in the Bible. In the very beginning, God restored Adam and Eve after they had sinned. Then, when Cain killed Abel, God had to raise up a new generation that would call on the name of the Lord (see Genesis 4). If one views the creation story as a restoration out of chaos (which I mentioned in chapter 2 as a possibility), then God restored something significant up to three times in the first four chapters of the Bible. He established a paradigm: He is the Restorer of lost inheritance. He is the God who gives us a future and a hope, even when it seems all has gone up in smoke.

Ruth and Naomi lost everything in Moab, both husbands and home. Ruth blindly followed Naomi, who had become bitter through loss. All Ruth knew was that God had knit her to Naomi. When Naomi returned to Bethlehem, Ruth went with her. The restoration process began to unfold, restoration not only of their relationships but also of their inheritance. Read the book of Ruth—what a powerful record of God the Restorer. Story after story in Scripture reveals God's nature as the Restorer of lives, relationships and inheritance.

Talk about a dark night of the soul! Job experienced one of the worst dark nights in all of recorded history:

> Now there was a day when his sons and daughters were eating and drinking wine in their oldest brother's house; and a messenger came to Job and said, "The oxen were plowing and the donkeys feeding beside them, when the Sabeans raided them and took them away—indeed they have killed the servants with the edge of the sword; and I alone have escaped to tell you!"
>
> While he was still speaking, another also came and said, "The fire of God fell from heaven and burned up the sheep and the servants, and consumed them; and I alone have escaped to tell you!"

While he was still speaking, another also came and said,
"The Chaldeans formed three bands, raided the camels and
took them away, yes, and killed the servants with the edge of
the sword; and I alone have escaped to tell you!"
While he was still speaking, another also came and said,
"Your sons and daughters were eating and drinking wine in
their oldest brother's house, and suddenly a great wind came
from across the wilderness and struck the four corners of the
house, and it fell on the young people, and they are dead; and
I alone have escaped to tell you!"

Job 1:13–19

With everything removed from him, Job must have ques-
tioned his very identity. Who *was* he now? He could no longer
be called "Father," because he had no children. Nor was he a
man of standing in his community, as he had been the day
before, because suddenly he had lost his wealth and his ability
to support himself. Everything by which he had been identified
was gone. Overnight he had become a charity case.

Yet it was Job who said that when God was finished trying
him, he would come forth as gold. In the Scripture quote that
follows, Job started off his deliberation by stating that he could
not find God. He said he looked in every direction, but could
not catch so much as a glimpse of Him. Job ended by saying
he was so completely in the dark that he could not even see
his hand in front of his face:

> I travel East looking for him—I find no one;
>   then West, but not a trace;
> I go North, but he's hidden his tracks;
>   then South, but not even a glimpse.
> But he knows where I am and what I've done.
>   He can cross-examine me all he wants, and I'll pass
>   the test
>   with honors.

> I've followed him closely, my feet in his footprints,
> 	not once swerving from his way.
> I've obeyed every word he's spoken,
> 	and not just obeyed his advice—I've treasured it.
> But he is singular and sovereign. Who can argue with
> 		him?
> 	He does what he wants, when he wants to.
> He'll complete in detail what he's decided about me,
> 	and whatever else he determines to do.
> Is it any wonder that I dread meeting him?
> 	Whenever I think about it, I get scared all over
> 		again.
> God makes my heart sink!
> 	God Almighty gives me the shudders!
> I'm completely in the dark,
> 	I can't see my hand in front of my face.
>
> 							Job 23:8–17, MESSAGE

But Job also knew that this season would end after its refining work on him was finished, and that restoration would come. Job knew God as the Restorer, and he held on tenaciously until his long night was over. Though he struggled with the overwhelming darkness, Job declared, "He knows the way that I take; when He has tested me, I shall come forth as gold" (Job 23:10).

God's heart is always to restore, to bring back to life, to reinstate, rebuild, reestablish, renovate and repair.

Those of us who have experienced significant losses and have come through them victoriously know firsthand this part of God's character. Others who are currently going through threatening experiences are just hanging on for dear life, hoping that God's Word is true. Their faith is being tested, and the test itself is part of the verification of their faith. True faith is faith that is tested.

Risky Business

A friend of mine brought me an article from the University of Michigan Medical School news magazine, *Medicine at Michigan*. The article caught my attention because of how it talks about the "eight-cell stage" of a human embryo:

> Inside the mother's body . . . the embryo divides to form two cells, then four cells, then eight. At the eight-cell stage, through a process scientists still don't understand, the embryo somehow activates its genes. From this point on, the embryo is on its own to follow its unique genetic destiny. If anything interferes with gene activation, the embryo will die.
>
> In the language of reproductive biology, it's called embryonic developmental competence, and it's a critical point where development often stops for reasons scientists don't understand. "Some eggs have what it takes to support the embryo's development past the eight-cell stage and some don't," Smith explains. "Most eggs will fertilize and the embryos will start to divide normally, but when they reach the eight-cell stage, the system sometimes breaks down and development stops."
>
> Exactly what an egg must have to make it possible for the embryo to turn on its genes, and how to tell which eggs have it, are two of the most important questions in developmental biology today, according to Smith. "We know this developmental time point is very important for the embryo's survival and that gene activation is regulated by maternal, or egg-derived, factors, but we don't understand how the transformation works," Smith says.[3]

What does this mean in relation to our present topic? In human embryonic development, it is at the eight-cell stage (eight meaning new beginning, new day, new gate or new door in Scripture) that the embryo is the most fragile, and that is just like us when we enter the new day. Our passage through the night is our most fragile, risky time. It is where we may abort the new because the process is too hard.

The article went on to say that only about 20 percent of the embryos make it to successful implantation in the uterine wall of the mother. Now *that* is fragility! Translating this embryonic phenomenon into the passage through the darkness into the new day, the eight-cell stage is the time when some people decide to jump ship or go no further in their walk with God. If they stop, they end up being frozen in time, never continuing their development unless they repent and change their minds. Their future as God planned it gets aborted.

Furthermore, the eight-cell stage is the time when the embryo's new identity is established because the DNA is being set. What transpires in us when we enter the new day? Our identity is transformed, tweaked, rearranged to fit the new day or era we are entering—so that we can be what God has called us to be in the new place.

No matter how hard the process becomes, I do not want to be a casualty of the night season, do you? I doubt it. Something in each one of us wants to make it all the way through to the prize. Paul declared his own intent in Philippians 3 when he noted that he was pressing toward the prize. To make it all the way through the night to the dawning of the new day, you and I must likewise enter into a "pressing." We need to persevere and never give up, even when everything inside us shouts, "It's too hard! Just give up!"

Passing through a Narrow Place

The number eight is linked with new things. In Scripture, that number represents both new things and gates. With something new, we must always pass through gates or doorways. It is the only way to get into the new season or the new thing. To move successfully through the narrowed, often dark passageway of a gate requires a new anointing. The eight-cell stage of an embryo is like a gateway to the next stage of growth—in other words, to a new thing. Passing from the old to the new can be risky business.

More often than not, we need to hang on for dear life during our spiritual "eight-cell stages," even if our faith is in tatters. We need to establish the fact that we *will* be restored—and more—in due time. We will not only be preserved from destruction, but we will step into a new identity.

The Need for Resolve

Consider Jacob again. Just before he entered his new day when God was going to restore him to his brother, Esau, and the rest of his family, he had to wrestle all night with the angel. Two things were at stake. First, his resolve, his determination. Would he persevere, wrestling through that dark night and intense battle until dawn? And second, would he give up his old name and make it through to the changing of his name and his identity? Would he humble himself so that God could visit him with grace and favor? Would he wrestle through to the new level of influence and authority that God was about to give to him?

Job went through the same process, but with a different set of circumstances. He had already lost everything, whereas Jacob faced the potential of losing everything if his reconciliation with Esau did not go well. I suspect that Job's challenge was far greater than Jacob's. Given his degree of loss, Job could have aborted the whole process by harboring bitterness toward men as well as anger toward God for what had happened. He could have failed to enter his new day.

Os Hillman, in an article called "The Black Hole," identified such times of intense darkness as times when God is building our "heat shield." He compared such times to John Glenn's initial reentry into the earth's atmosphere in the early days of the space program. No one knew for sure that his capsule's heat shield would withstand the incredible temperatures it must pass through to bring Glenn safely back home. Hillman wrote,

> There was a blackout period for several minutes in which mission control had no radio contact. He was in the "black hole." It was a tense time. Either he would make it through, or the spacecraft would burn up in the atmosphere. There were several minutes of silence that seemed like an eternity. Then, mission control shouted with joy when they reestablished contact with the spacecraft. It was a time of rejoicing.
>
> Have you ever had a time when you were in a spiritual black hole in your life? I have. The pressure was unbearable. No sense of God's presence. No sense of anything going on around me. God was about as far away as the man in the moon—at least from my perspective. I think every Christian who is called to make a significant difference in his world experiences times like these. These are the times when we question the reality of God, the love of God, the personal care of God. And He demonstrates to us that He was there all the time. These are "faith experiences" that God does in every person who is called to a higher level of relationship with Him. These times are needful in order to know that we have the "heat shield" that can withstand the incredible heat that comes when we follow Him with a whole heart—a heart that is radical in a commitment to fully follow His ways (see 1 Kings 19:21).[4]

As we know, both Jacob and Job passed their tests. Their "heat shields" of faith held strong. Jacob had to persevere through a dark and trying night, but in the morning a new day dawned in his life. Job was honest about his suffering, but he did not abort the new, restored life that God lavished on him. He also entered his new day and fulfilled the purposes for which God had created him.

For both, their latter days were more blessed than their earlier, well-blessed days. They saw God restore their future, their hope, their inheritance—all that they needed. God used their darkest hours as powerful spiritual weapons that ushered in a new anointing. It was worth it.

6

The Battle of Wills

It was a bad day in heaven, a crisis of unparalleled propor-
tions. Something horrible, something downright chilling
had just happened. Lucifer had made up his mind that he
was just as capable as God.

He was, in fact, a remarkably magnificent being, possessing
physical beauty, wisdom and intelligence. God had entrusted
the administration of His government in heaven to him. Lucifer covered the throne, the governmental center of heaven,
and he orchestrated the heavenly worship that surrounded
the sovereign God.

In a prophetic passage that most people believe applies to
Lucifer, Ezekiel writes:

Thus says the Lord GOD:

"You were the seal of perfection,
Full of wisdom and perfect in beauty.

You were in Eden, the garden of God;
Every precious stone was your covering:
The sardius, topaz, and diamond,
Beryl, onyx, and jasper,
Sapphire, turquoise, and emerald with gold.
The workmanship of your timbrels and pipes
Was prepared for you on the day you were created.
You were the anointed cherub who covers;
I established you;
You were on the holy mountain of God;
You walked back and forth in the midst of fiery stones.
You were perfect in your ways from the day you were
      created,
Till iniquity was found in you.

Ezekiel 28:12–15

Next to God, Lucifer's position was the highest in heaven. He was the chief of all created beings. In the government of God, he had been positioned as ruler over the creation of God.[1]

As a created being, Lucifer was subject to the will of the One who created him. As long as there was one will, heaven hummed along with glorious unity. As long as Lucifer acknowledged that one will as supreme, he remained perfect in all his ways (see Ezekiel 28:15).

A fundamental distinguishing characteristic of God is that He gives His subjects freedom of will, the freedom to choose whether or not they will follow Him. He does not desire puppets. He is looking for followers who will love and embrace Him from their hearts. He has invited His created beings to follow Him. It is an invitation, not a conscription. His Son, Jesus, reflected this liberty:

When He had called the people to Himself, with His disciples also, He said to them, "Whoever desires to come after Me, let him deny himself, and take up his cross, and follow Me. For whoever desires to save his life will lose it, but whoever loses his life for My sake and the gospel's will save it. For what will it profit a man if he gains the whole world, and loses his own soul? Or what will a man give in exchange for his soul?"

Mark 8:34–37

Just as He does with us, God gave Lucifer, the chief angelic being in heaven, the right to choose. God did not impose His divine will on him. If Lucifer chose rightly, aligning himself with God, he would flourish. If not, he would diminish greatly.

On that dreadful day in heaven, something had turned dark in Lucifer's heart. That day marked the discovery of iniquity in the heart of Lucifer (see Ezekiel 28:15). What was the iniquity? It was the *merchandising* of the authority God had given him. Merchandising was Lucifer's downfall.

Merchandising means turning the flow of that which passes through your hands (such as money, power, fame, achievement or glory) toward yourself in a selfish, self-centered and corrupted way. It is using for yourself that which you have been given for the sake of building up someone else. One synonym for *merchandising* is *trading*. A merchandiser takes what he has been given and trades or exchanges it for personal profit. Other terms for *merchandising* are *trafficking* or *wheeling and dealing*. Those imply a hidden, dark motive. Lucifer traded his worship of God for the worship of self. He took what God had given him—the freedom to flourish as the covering angelic being over the throne—and he traded that freedom to, in essence, "work for himself." He betrayed the One who had given him authority.

Lucifer decided that instead of directing the worship from other spirit beings back to God, he would retain some of that worship for himself. He was a marvelous being, and he ruled with excellence. Everything about him was glorious. Why should he not get some of the glory? Why should he stand by,

87

watching God get all of the honor? Pride filled his heart, and he rebelled. "By the abundance of your trading you became filled with violence within, and you sinned" (Ezekiel 28:16).

Alas, now instead of one will in heaven, there were two. God judged Lucifer that day and removed him from heaven:

> "Therefore I cast you as a profane thing
> Out of the mountain of God;
> And I destroyed you, O covering cherub,
> From the midst of the fiery stones.
> Your heart was lifted up because of your beauty;
> You corrupted your wisdom for the sake of your
>   splendor;
> I cast you to the ground,
> I laid you before kings,
> That they might gaze at you.
> You defiled your sanctuaries
> By the multitude of your iniquities,
> By the iniquity of your trading."
>
> Ezekiel 28:16–18

This one event marked the beginning of darkness, evil and sin. A new dynamic had been released. An alternative will had been unleashed on the world, a dark, sinister, evil will that caused a perfect creation to go awry. From that day forward, there was no longer one will, but two wills in the universe—(1) God's will, and (2) any will contrary to God's will. Because there could not be two wills (two governments) coexisting in God's Kingdom in heaven, Lucifer was cast out of heaven to the earth.

Isaiah spoke about this incident in a parallel passage.

> How you are fallen from heaven,
> O Lucifer, son of the morning!
> How you are cut down to the ground,

You who weakened the nations!
For you have said in your heart:
"I will ascend into heaven,
I will exalt my throne above the stars of God;
I will also sit on the mount of the congregation
On the farthest sides of the north;
I will ascend above the heights of the clouds,
I will be like the Most High."
Yet you shall be brought down to Sheol,
To the lowest depths of the Pit.

Isaiah 14:12-15

Worship, the Heart of the Issue

The fundamental problem was that Lucifer felt he was equal with God, so he decided he would no longer subject himself to God. He interposed a new will into the equation—his own. In his own eyes, he was now like God, which meant that he worshiped himself.

Worship was the heart of the issue. To worship is to bow down, to yield to, to love and therefore serve someone with abandonment. It means placing someone or something at the center of one's life and allowing the object of worship to govern decisions.

Misdirected worship thus becomes the core of sin, because sin demonstrates subjection to something other than God. Adam and Eve's Fall could be called a worship issue. They, like Lucifer, bowed down to the will of someone other than God—their own wills. God had told them not to eat of the Tree of Knowledge of Good and Evil. In that failure, they ultimately were demonstrating their belief that they knew better than God. Their belief about what would lead them to life became different than God's, so their choice contradicted God's directions to them. These failings of the earliest created

89

beings made it necessary for God to operate as a restoring, redemptive God.

Worship is at the heart of spiritual darkness as well as light. The primary difference between the light and the darkness is simple: Who or what is worshiped—who or what is determining the decisions we make? This basic challenge confronts us day in and day out—to whom or to what will we bow down? We have a choice about whose will to align with, God's will or some other will antagonistic to God's will, such as the will of Satan or of someone whom he has influenced.

A New Perspective

We talked about Job's darkest hours in the previous chapter. I wonder if the reason Job made it all the way through his dark night was because of the way he set his heart in the beginning, when the tragedies first unfolded. When he heard the bad news of the total destruction of his family and possessions, Job entered his dark night. Amazingly, he entered it *worshiping*:

> *Then Job arose, tore his robe, and shaved his head; and he fell to the ground and worshiped.* And he said:
> "Naked I came from my mother's womb,
> And naked shall I return there.
> The LORD gave, and the LORD has taken away;
> Blessed be the name of the LORD."
> In all this Job did not sin nor charge God with wrong.
>
> Job 1:20–22, emphasis added

Ultimately, Job faced a worship issue. And ultimately, he chose to worship God and demonstrate his faith in Him. Faith and worship belong together. When they part ways, God's purposes are thwarted. What was the underlying problem with Eve and then Adam? It was worship. That was the problem with Cain also.

Worship is about far more than a certain type of music or what we do in church. It is a heart attitude, a stance toward God, an obedience issue. Worship is being totally sold out to the One who "owns" us, giving ourselves away to someone or something we think is greater than ourselves. It is single-hearted devotion.

One meaning of the Hebrew word for worship is "to lick like a dog." I love that meaning because it so vividly paints a fitting picture. A dog who is totally yielded to his master overwhelms his master with undivided attention and total obedience. When the master comes home, the dog greets his master excitedly, licking his face. The dog is consumed with his master.

Our hardest times challenge you and me to go the heart of the matter, to worship. Can you do it? Can I? Will you do it? Will I? The answer to this question sets our future course and ultimately determines our end—for good or for evil.

We Need a Savior

How easy it sounds to say, "Align with God's will, and your life will be blessed." How difficult it can be in real life, when the dark night seems endless. Without the saving grace of Jesus, we cannot take the first step away from this stifling, thick fog of darkness toward God's light, which is freedom from darkness. He also delivers us from the inevitable results of our sinful choices, places where we have taken a wrong turn. Even in the darkest places, He brings His light:

> The cords and sorrows of death were around me, and the terrors of Sheol (the place of the dead) had laid hold of me; I suffered anguish and grief (trouble and sorrow).
>
> Then called I upon the name of the Lord: O Lord, I beseech You, save my life and deliver me!
>
> Gracious is the Lord, and [rigidly] righteous; yes, our God is merciful.
>
> The Lord preserves the simple; I was brought low, and He helped and saved me.

Return to your rest, O my soul, for the Lord has dealt boun-
tifully with you.
For You have delivered my life from death, my eyes from
tears, and my feet from stumbling and falling.

Psalm 116:3–8, AMP

Darkness will attach itself to anything that is not yet light in
us, to that which is broken, unhealed or inherited (as in iniquitous generational issues and weaknesses)—it will attach itself
to any sin. When you experience a dark night, it is important
to ask God to expose the places in your soul that have not yet
been filled with His light. "He shines a spotlight into caves of
darkness, hauls deepest darkness into the noonday sun" (Job
12:22, MESSAGE). He will keep shining His light into the dark
corners of your heart until you yourself can see what is deep
inside. Then you can turn it over to Him for transformation.
(Even if your dark times are brought on by things someone else
does that affect you directly or indirectly, God can use such
external assaults to transform you into His likeness.)

The process of exposing the darkness within may be uncomfortable, but it will be worth it. This is the death and resurrection process. This is the working out of the salvation of
your soul. This is your time to grow in living by faith. This is
true discipleship.

Like it or not, the deepest changes occur in the middle of
the deepest, darkest night seasons. God allows it to happen this
way because He loves you (see Hebrews 12:5–7 and Proverbs
3:11–12).

Your Own Experience

In your personal dark night of the soul, the lights are turned off
to force you into the new day of freedom. If you have walked

with God for very many years, you already know that this can happen in all sorts of ways, and it certainly will happen more than once.

Everything that grows changes by degrees over time. It is the same with your spirit and your soul. Your spirit embraced the light of God most readily. But your soul (your intellect, emotions and will) needs to catch up to the faster growth of your spirit. When your soul falls behind, not only are you a lopsided person inside, but you end up in a struggle. It is the classic struggle we just talked about between two wills—yours and God's. Sometimes Satan inserts himself into the battle as well. What happens when another will clashes with God's will? The darkness begins to descend.

Sometimes the source of your "dark night" seems to lie outside yourself—perhaps caused by circumstances external to your will. When your personal decisions are not the root of your problems, the only way out of the trouble is to proceed straight through the middle, laying down your will in favor of God's. Remember Job.

As I noted in chapter 3, your darkness is usually the result of your bowing down to another will, even if you did not know what you were doing. Do not waste your time worrying about who or what is to blame. Get busy asking God for light and understanding. Ask Him for the ability to accept the process even as you move toward the light with His help. Consider this familiar passage of Scripture in the Amplified version:

> Do not fret or have any anxiety about anything, but in every circumstance and in everything, by prayer and petition (definite requests), with thanksgiving, continue to make your wants known to God.
>
> And God's peace [shall be yours, that tranquil state of a soul assured of its salvation through Christ, and so fearing nothing from God and being content with its earthly lot of whatever

THE OVERCOMER'S ANOINTING

sort that is, that peace] which transcends all understanding
shall garrison and mount guard over your hearts and minds
in Christ Jesus.

Philippians 4:6–7, AMP

Every time, you will discover that God wants to help you
even more than you want to be helped. He is the One who
has orchestrated your circumstances so that you would
ask for His saving help. Always, He makes the day follow
the night. Always, He is your Savior, saving you from your
darkness-causing sin. "For You will save the humble people,
but will bring down haughty looks. For You will light my
lamp; the LORD my God will enlighten my darkness" (Psalm
18:27–28).

What to Look For

How do you know that God is trying to uncover something
in you for the purpose of transformation?

You know when you find yourself in darkness—again—and
it is not the first time. You may not have felt this particular
darkness for years, but when you find yourself in it, you can
interpret it to mean that God is saying, *It is time. I want to remove the cause of this darkness. I want you to see the thing that
causes you to go into fear or anger or hurt or rebellion. I want
to shine My light on it. I want to save you from it.*

He wants you to press through with His help. He will connect you with other people or resources that are potentially
part of His provision for you. For your part, just be honest with
Him and with yourself. Make an effort to acknowledge His
lordship over your life. Praise Him, even if your effort seems
puny. Talk to someone or journal about what you are going
through. Pour out your heart to God. "Trust in Him at all times,
you people; pour out your heart before Him; God is a refuge

for us" (Psalm 62:8). I find it helpful to journal extensively at these times, writing out my "complaints," my dilemmas and my questions for the Lord.

Remind yourself of the promises of God, especially the ones He has highlighted to you personally. As you cooperate with Him, you will be working out your salvation in very concrete and practical ways (see Philippians 2:12). You will be transformed by the renewal of your mind (see Romans 12:2 and Philippians 3:14–15). As you are increasingly able to align your will with God's will, the result will be lightness of heart, peace and more strength than you knew was available. With His ever-available help, you will press through your dark night. You will be an overcomer. You will have won another round in the battle of wills.

> May God himself, the God who makes everything holy and whole, make you holy and whole, put you together—spirit, soul, and body—and keep you fit for the coming of our Master, Jesus Christ. The One who called you is completely dependable. If he said it, he'll do it!
>
> 1 Thessalonians 5:23–24, MESSAGE

A Test of Your Allegiance

I read a story about a football player named Brian Kisabeth, who played for the University of Buffalo in Buffalo, New York. He was potentially an outstanding player. Yet every season through his senior year, he did not get to play because of changes in team positions or injuries that occurred before the football season even began. Finally, when he was in graduate school, his turn to play finally came. This time, would he make it to the opening game of the season and actually play in it? After all the previous years, he wondered if he would ever put on his uniform. Read what he said:

I rehabbed all summer and I finished up my rehab at the end of that season and I couldn't wait for spring ball, couldn't wait to get back into it, learning tight end again. And then I hurt it in camp again [his knee ligament] and it was like, "I don't know if I can do this again." I tried to stay positive. I graduated and am in graduate school right now [international business], and that helped me come back.[2]

The whole situation severely tested Kisabeth's resolve. He decided to stay in the running. He worked through what was important to him. He stayed true to his goal of playing football for the University of Buffalo. As a first-year graduate student, he caught the first touchdown of his first game. After three seasons of sitting on the sidelines and two knee surgeries, he prevailed.

Although not a "spiritual" example, this is a picture of how our allegiance to a cause or goal can be tested by a dark night of the soul. Kisabeth stayed with his original decision. Why had he gone to the University of Buffalo in the first place? Would he stay until he accomplished his goal?

Jesus said that if you follow (worship) Him, you will find life. Will you stick with Him? Or will you waver when the going gets tough? A test of your allegiance will come, particularly when you enter the evening and the dark hours of your new day.

Will you follow Jesus faithfully, or will you hang back in disillusionment, anger or frustration, deciding that your way, your will, is better? Will you worship your own evaluation of the situation and follow your own conclusions? Or will you, like Job, choose to stick with God—even express heartfelt worship to Him—whether your life is light or dark? Can you trust and worship God when it appears that His blessings have been obliterated?

You know the saying "two is better than one"? In *this* case two—two wills—is *not* better than one. God alone is our Lord, and that means we must align ourselves with His will alone.

It is not too late. The night is young!

7

The Struggle to Believe

I do not need to tell you that it can be a struggle to maintain your trust in God, especially in the midst of a dark night of the soul. When darkness descends in your life, you wonder sometimes if you will make it at all. Your faith wobbles. You grapple with fears and doubts. If you yield to the bitterness of hope deferred (as I did when I lost half of my close family in the same month), your doubts are likely to turn into unbelief. Unbelief was the prevailing sin of the Israelites when they were in the wilderness, and we do not want to make it ours.

The word *unbelief* is interpreted as "disobedience" in one translation of the Bible:

> It still remains that some will enter that rest, and those who formerly had the gospel preached to them did not go in, because of their disobedience. Therefore God again set a certain day, calling it Today, when a long time later he spoke through David,

as was said before: "Today, if you hear his voice, do not harden your hearts." For if Joshua had given them rest, God would not have spoken later about another day. There remains, then, a Sabbath-rest for the people of God; for anyone who enters God's rest also rests from his own work, just as God did from his. Let us, therefore, make every effort to enter that rest, so that no one will fall by following their example of disobedience.

Hebrews 4:6–11, NIV

The children of Israel's disobedience prevented them from entering not only the Promised Land, but also from entering the place of rest. Because they disbelieved God's promises, they did not acquire those promises or live to see their fulfillment.

Only those who kept pressing on and working hard to advance could possess the land and enter their much-deserved rest. They completed their job successfully, and at last they walked into the place God had promised them. Now they could relax, settle down and cease striving. There is a time to work hard and press on to all that God has for us, and there is a time to rest once we have arrived.

Unbelief is sin because it is the manifestation of a will independent of and contradictory to God's will. You could say that unbelief is belief that has been broken, marred or bent. Something "off" happens, and you get tripped up in your beliefs.

This idea of unbelief being bent or warped belief is particularly clear in the biblical incident in which the townspeople of Jesus' hometown, Nazareth, were "offended" in Him when He worked miracles. According to *Strong's Concordance*, the word *offended* in that context means that they were tripped up by something. The root word used means "to bend." Their faith became bent; no longer was it straight. They had allowed their doubts about Jesus' divine powers—born of their over-familiarity with Him as their fellow Nazarene—to be warped into unbelief.

When the Sabbath had come, He began to teach in the synagogue. And many hearing Him were astonished, saying, "Where did this Man get these things? And what wisdom is this which is given to Him, that such mighty works are performed by His hands! Is this not the carpenter, the Son of Mary, and brother of James, Joses, Judas, and Simon? And are not His sisters here with us?" So they were offended at Him.

But Jesus said to them, "A prophet is not without honor except in his own country, among his own relatives, and in his own house." Now He could do no mighty work there, except that He laid His hands on a few sick people and healed them. And He marveled because of their unbelief. Then He went about the villages in a circuit, teaching.

Mark 6:2–6

Jesus was unable to work many miracles in Nazareth because His own people did not believe He could perform miracles. They knew Him too well—and yet they did not know Him at all.

Sometimes it can be a challenge to believe. When summer changes to fall, in our church we dedicate our children to the Lord for their school year. We lay hands on them and pray the prayer of faith over them. We speak into their destiny as students. During one of these dedicatory services, I talked briefly about Josiah, the boy-king of Israel, who was anointed as king when he was only eight years old. I invited all of the eight-year-olds to stand up. I then asked them if they could imagine becoming the president of the United States at their age or even the principal of their school. They all shook their heads no, and a couple of them spoke up, saying, "No way!" I looked them over, assessing their size, maturity, education and level of experience. What would I have thought if I had been there when Josiah was chosen as king? Most definitely, I would have been tempted toward unbelief. How could it ever

101

be God's will to allow a child to rule a nation? By my standards, it would not make sense.

Even in less obvious situations, you and I are tempted to doubt and then to disbelieve. I am sure you can think of a time when you missed an awesome breakthrough or even a miracle because you had become too familiar with the vessel through whom it was meant to come. Can you receive ministry from a child? Have you become too familiar with your pastor, other leaders, your family or friends? Can you receive a miracle from the prayers of a convicted murderer?

I once visited a prison in Argentina where many of the prisoners had become Christians. They had become a massive prayer cell for outside ministries, individuals and churches all around the world. Several of the prisoners laid their hands on me and prayed for me, and I can attest to a mighty impartation. Those men are lights in the darkness, and the darkness around them cannot put out their God-given light. They had to choose to believe that God could use them just as much as I had to choose to receive from them. Belief opened the doors of opportunity, even in the locked-down environment of the prison. Unbelief would have allowed the darkness to prevail.

No Excuse for Unbelief

If we refuse to believe, no excuse will suffice to gain God's grace. If we refuse to believe, we will remain in darkness. Unbelief is disobedience. If we yield to unbelief and do not walk in the light because of it, we will be further cut off from His light and life. We will have chosen to walk the dark path.

To believe is a choice, and it leads to obedience, which is also a choice. If only we could remember how simple this is when we are stumbling around in the darkness! If we believe, light will shine on our path. God is light, and Jesus is the Light of the world. In Him there is no darkness, there is no shadow of turning (see James 1:17). No bending or warping, either. If you believe in God, you will be filled with light. If you believe in His Word, you will see what to do. The Light will show you the way, and it will also expose the traps that have been laid to capture you and trip you up, especially those dark snares of unbelief.

Too often, people are snared by unbelief when they play the blame card, palming off their doubts by saying, "Somebody hurt me." "My father abused me." "My pastor offended me." "My husband did something to me." "My wife wouldn't let me do something I thought I should do." Or they say, "I couldn't help it. That's just the way I am, the way my family is. I'm too busy to figure it out or to change it."

I am sorry—no excuses will do. God has a bottom line, and it is called "belief." Belief listens, hears, obeys and acts promptly. It does not make excuses, pretend to be deaf, spurn commands or hang around waiting for someone else to do the heavy lifting. Belief is a pearl of great price, and it will be worth everything we have to sacrifice for it.

I remember a time when I chose outright *not* to believe. I was too offended at God. I was angry and bitter about the life He had given me. I would not believe His Word. My unbelief led me straight into disobedience, and my willful disobedience cut me off from the life that God wanted me to enjoy.

The consequence of my unbelief and disobedience was spiritual death. My independence from God and my rebellion against Him felt pleasant for a season, but after a while my life became extremely difficult. I felt as if I lived in a dark and tormented place. I lost my way, spiraling down into a dark pit until I finally cried out, "I've had enough, God! I need You! Show me how to get back on the path." He did.

One direct result of my side trip into darkness was that I realized how important it is to avoid being offended and angry with God. He knows what He is doing. He is God, and He cares about each one of us as only a loving heavenly Father can do.

Together with me, read and agree with what the writer of the letter to the Hebrews advised:

> Beware, brethren, lest there be in any of you an evil heart of unbelief in departing from the living God; but exhort one another daily, while it is called "Today," lest any of you be hardened through the deceitfulness of sin. For we have become partakers of Christ if we hold the beginning of our confidence steadfast to the end, while it is said:
> "Today, if you will hear His voice,
> Do not harden your hearts as in the rebellion."
> For who, having heard, rebelled? Indeed, was it not all who came out of Egypt, led by Moses? Now with whom was He angry forty years? Was it not with those who sinned, whose corpses fell in the wilderness? And to whom did He swear that they would not enter His rest, but to those who did not obey? So we see that they could not enter in because of unbelief.

Hebrews 3:12–19

When you are traversing your night season, watch out for those places where your will comes into conflict with God's will and threatens to turn into the sin of unbelief. You must choose—once, twice, repeatedly—to obey His will, if you expect to walk out of your night season into the break of day.

The very nature of darkness makes it even more important to choose to walk by faith, not by sight. Do not become offended at God for allowing you to traverse such a dark time. Do not be like Job's wife, who urged him to curse God: "His wife said to him, 'Are you still holding on to your integrity? Curse God and die!'" (Job 2:9, NIV).

Practically speaking, you *will* struggle with doubts. They may fill your heart and mind with raging storms. But I am here to tell you that *doubting is not the same as unbelief.* If you can distinguish between doubt and unbelief, you can keep yourself from stepping over the line into unbelief, with all of its hazardous results: waywardness, disobedient defiance, obstinacy. And if you do step over the line, you can confess and repent, crying out to God like the man in the gospel of Mark who cried out to Jesus, "I don't believe, but I want to believe! Help me, Lord!" (see Mark 9:24).

God will help you believe. The struggle is the greatest in the middle of the dark night. That is when you and I are the most strongly tempted to sin. Captured with myriad doubts, we wrestle and try not to fall prey to unbelief. Yet as Philippians 2:13 says, God works in you and me "both to will and to do for His good pleasure."

Before you entered into your dark place, what did God say to you? That prophetic word is still true. That word has not failed, and its purpose is to give you the faith to make it all the way through the night. It was never meant to be fulfilled immediately, but sometimes we look for the light of day just when darkness is falling. Sometimes we forget that a new day begins with the evening. Like you, I have often forgotten about the darkness that must follow a word of promise.

God gives a prophetic word to you so that you will know where you are headed—and so that you can develop the persistence you need to press through the dark night that lies between where you are now and where you will be eventually. He wants you to press in, labor hard and work to enter into the promise. (I wrote an entire book, *Taking On Goliath*, about this effort of pressing in.)

In the end, traversing the darkness will be worth it. With the fulfillment of God's promise and with rest comes joy. You will have made it through all of the temptation, through the dark night of doubts and the potential for unbelief. The break of day will be the time to celebrate. The work of your hard night will be finished.

But—What about Doubt?

Most of us struggle with doubt. The Israelites took their doubts all the way over into unbelief because they refused to obey God in spite of the ways He had revealed His will to them. In the remainder of this chapter, I want to take a good, hard look at doubt. If we can get a handle on the ins and outs of doubt, we can overcome it. We can be too hard on doubt, and we can be too soft on it. We need to find the middle ground.

Biblically, doubt itself is a halfway stage. Doubt is halfway to unbelief; it is also halfway to believing. When you are in doubt about something, you can still change your mind. There is no such thing as being in "total doubt," unless you are already talking about unbelief.

As I was working on this chapter, I came across a book by Os Guinness called *God in the Dark*. I gleaned much from his second chapter, "Dare to Doubt." He notes that the Latin word for doubt is *dubitare*, meaning "to hesitate or to have reservations"—in other words, to be of two minds. Doubt is not quite the same as unbelief, although both are negative states of mind. As undesirable as unbelief may be, it is nevertheless a single-minded state of mind and heart. Just as to believe means you are of one mind about trusting somebody or something, to disbelieve means you are, in fact, still of one mind—but about mistrusting someone or something that you are fully against.

To doubt, however, means wavering between the two, believing and disbelieving at the same time. A doubter is double-minded and unsure. A doubter might end up going over into unbelief. Doubt puts you on the horns of a dilemma. Your heart is divided when you doubt.

In one of his psalms, David said, "Unite my heart" (Psalm 86:11). He was saying, "My heart is split in two; it is divided. So my prayer, God, is that You will settle the war in my heart. Make me single-hearted in faith. May I fear Your name; so that I am of one heart and therefore of one mind."

In his book, Guinness lists some of the different phrases in different languages that express the two wills of doubt. To English speakers, doubt is "having a foot in both camps." To the Chinese, it is "having a foot in two boats." Two groups of Andes Indians say it is "thinking two things" or "having two thoughts." In Guatemala, the Kekchi Indians say the man who doubts is "the man whose heart is made two." The Navajo Indians say, "that which is two with him."[1]

In Greek, the language of the New Testament, the five words that are translated "doubt" express the meaning of ambivalence or double-mindedness. Let's examine each of these words, all of which carry particular nuances of the same idea—two wills or two minds.[2]

Dipsukos refers to a person who is chronically double-minded. It is used in this familiar passage:

> But let him ask in faith, with no doubting, for he who doubts is like a wave of the sea driven and tossed by the wind. For let not that man suppose that he will receive anything from the Lord; he is a double-minded man, unstable in all his ways.
>
> James 1:6–8

Other English translations of verse 8 express *dipsukos* in various ways: "adrift at sea, keeping all your options open" (MESSAGE); "unstable in all he does" (NIV); "Such doubters are thinking two different things at the same time, and they cannot decide about anything they do" (NCV); "A person who has doubts is thinking about two different things at the same time and can't make up his mind about anything" (GOD'S WORD); "every decision you then make will be uncertain, as you turn first this way, and then that" (TLB); "a two-souled man [is] unstable in all his ways" (YLT); "such a one is a man of two minds, undecided in every step he takes" (WEYMOUTH).

Diakrino, the second Greek word, is a stronger word for doubt and means "to cut in two or separate." This term conveys an inner state torn between various opinions to the point that a person cannot make up his or her mind. Jesus used this word when He talked to His disciples about mountain-moving faith:

> So Jesus answered and said to them, "Have faith in God. For assuredly, I say to you, whoever says to this mountain, 'Be removed and be cast into the sea,' and does not *doubt* in his heart, but believes that those things he says will be done, he will have whatever he says."
>
> Mark 11:22–23, emphasis added

Meteorizo, the third Greek word for doubt, means "to raise or suspend" (like a meteor, which shares the root word). This kind of doubt is suspended in air, lifted up in the air, unsettled, restless, anxious and tense. The word can also imply being hung up about something. Here it is in scriptural context:

> Consider the lilies, how they grow: they neither toil nor spin; and yet I say to you, even Solomon in all his glory was not arrayed like one of these. If then God so clothes the grass, which today is in the field and tomorrow is thrown into the oven, how much more will He clothe you, O you of little faith?
>
> And do not seek what you should eat or what you should drink, nor *have an anxious mind*.
>
> Luke 12:27–29, emphasis added

Dialogizomai, the fourth Greek word, refers to an inner dialogue, the debate of a person reasoning with himself or herself. When I doubt, I internally argue or reason. I go back and forth in my mind. Jesus used this word with the disciples after His resurrection.

> Jesus Himself stood in the midst of them, and said to them, "Peace to you." But they were terrified and frightened, and supposed they had seen a spirit. And He said to them, "Why are you troubled? And *why do doubts arise in your hearts*? Behold My hands and My feet, that it is I Myself. Handle Me and see, for a spirit does not have flesh and bones as you see I have."
>
> Luke 24:36–39, emphasis added

An internal dialogue was transpiring in the disciples' minds. They were asking themselves, *How could this be the same Jesus who died? Is He alive? Is He dead?* Their internal debate was intense.

Distazo is the fifth and last Greek word we will look at. It means "to hang back," "hesitate" or "falter," "to vacillate." Peter's problem with walking to Jesus on the water was that he hesitated between two opinions. He entertained reservations and started to sink. "And immediately Jesus stretched out His hand and caught him, and said to him, 'O you of little faith, why did you doubt?'" (Matthew 14:31).

Do Not Allow Doubt to Grow in the Dark

In essence, we could say that doubt is when you are torn between options and unable to make up your mind. You are up in the air over something and not sure which side to come down on; you are debating with yourself, hanging back and weighing up your reservations.

Genuine faith is unreserved in its commitment. Doubt has reservations. Faith has no reservations. Faith steps forward; doubt hangs back. Doubt holds itself open to every possibility, but it is reluctant to close on any. Doubt will not make up its mind.

When we are dealing with darkness, doubt rushes in. In dark and difficult times, doubt will be a bigger problem than outright unbelief, and doubt can be slippery to grab hold of. When we are grappling with doubt, we often struggle with self-condemnation. We might even accuse ourselves of not believing. But, at least for a long time, unbelief is *not* really our problem. Doubt is. We are of two minds. And we are anxious about it. But having two minds is not the same as having made up our mind to disbelieve.

Doubt, as I said earlier, can grow into unbelief, which is a willful refusal to believe and which is outright disobedience. Unbelief is a deliberate choice, like the Israelites' decision to disobey when God had clearly told them what they were supposed to do. Unbelief is a state of mind that is closed against God, with disobedience at its core. It is the sin of Lucifer, who inserted another will into God's universe.

When we face a long, dark night, one of our biggest challenges will be preventing doubt from growing into unbelief. As we just learned in our brief study of the five biblical Greek words for doubt, our overriding challenge will be to strive to remain of one mind—God's mind. Our challenge may be daunting at times as we wrestle with doubts (hesitations, faltering, reservations, ambivalence) and as we debate within ourselves, feeling torn in two and suspended up in the air.

Take it from someone who has wrestled through her share of doubts, though—when God allows you to descend into a dark night, do not doubt His love. Do not question His methods. Even if you must repeat it many times a day, keep telling yourself the truth: "God is good. I belong to Him, so this trial must be for my good and the good of others. I choose to acknowledge Him as my one Lord. I trust Him. I worship Him."

When whatever darkness you are facing is intense, doubt will usually become correspondingly intense. Ask God to keep you single-minded in your devotion to Him. Ask Him to help you see double-mindedness when it starts to arise.

As we move closer to the end of time, darkness will escalate. You and I will have to contend with demonic powers that we have never before faced. It is imperative that we learn to overcome, understanding the times and seasons as they appear in our own lives. Each one of us will need to contend for the Kingdom of God. We will need to be firm with ourselves and firm with the enemy, remembering that "From the days of John the Baptist until now, the kingdom of heaven has been forcefully advancing, and forceful men lay hold of it" (Matthew 11:12, NIV). We will need to be overcomers.

The narrow path of the overcomer is a single lane wide. We need to keep moving toward the light, with our faces set like a flint, not vacillating between two directions. The overcomer's path leads us from faith to faith, strength to strength and glory to glory!

8

The Voice

Emerging from the darkest part of the night and arriving at the 3:00 A.M. watch positions you for the emergence of the new day. You do not come through the "third watch" (midnight to 3:00 A.M.) unscathed by your experience of the long night, but you do come through it stronger. Neither do you come into the quiet, "wee hours" of the morning silently. Rather, you come into this portion of your journey with the invigorated, confident *voice* of one fortified with new authority by the tests and trials of the darkness.

Now that you have attained a more authoritative standing through your experience of the darkness, your earned authority, your voice, cannot remain silent. You must speak in order to break out of the night, to break off the hindrances and temptations that try to imprison you in the night and to declare what God intends to happen. Your voice, pummeled by doubts and questions in the midnight hour, has now emerged stronger and it is coupled with a new heart, as well as a transformed mind. Passing through the darkest part of the night has victoriously transformed the voice with which you now speak. You will now speak with new power, wisdom and influence. For the daylight, the glory of the morning, to break forth, your voice must speak.

A New Sound of Authority

Your voice has a new sound to it. Now it will no longer speak forth empty words. Now it can speak words impregnated with new power and authority—gained through overcoming in the midnight hour. It can speak from a heart moved by fresh compassion—forged through personal suffering. It can speak from a mind transformed to operate out of new paradigms.

Stripped of unnecessary trappings, your new voice stands ready for action. The midnight hour dealt a death blow to your old voice when you surrendered to God everything that had no place in the new day. New maps are emerging that lead the way in uncharted territory, and your transformed voice will begin to call forth that which is not as though it were (see Romans 4:17). This new voice of yours will break off the depression, despair, hopelessness, oppression and weariness that resulted from the bleakness of the dark night. It will birth a new joy and rejoicing, as well as calling forth the opening of the gates or doors to new places.

Those who possess powerful voices have faced and walked through the dark night of their soul for the purpose of being reshaped and transformed for the days ahead. They live out their lives listening to an inner Voice—God's Voice—that impassions them to persevere through every obstacle. Stephen Covey regards a person's voice as "a combination of vision, passion, discipline and conscience, with vision being the goal that one directs all of his or her efforts to achieve."[1]

Paradoxically, new *vision* has emerged from the blindness of your dark night—new goals and new hope in the possibilities that lie ahead. Blind though you are in the dark, sometimes that very darkness causes you to look more vigilantly for the answers you long for. Leaving behind any tendency to remain in the dark like a victim of paralysis, you gather new energy as the darkness fades into dawn. You are awake, ready, willing to sacrifice further if necessary. Now you can build on the foundation the night season has provided for you.

What Is Your Voice?

Your voice is so important that I have dedicated this entire chapter to it. I appreciate what Covey says about a person's voice, which he sees as one's unique personal significance. He defines your voice as your calling, your soul's code.[2] It has the power to transform whatever lies within your sphere of authority and influence. Your voice is integrally tied to your identity. In fact, Covey states that "identity is destiny,"[3] so your voice is who you are. Your voice determines how you will leverage your identity within your sphere of assignment, which is that task, calling or ministry that God has charged you with and given you the responsibility to fulfill.

Your voice's influence can have amazing longevity. Consider St. John of the Cross and Teresa of Avila, who both lived hundreds of years ago. Their voices still speak to us today because of the magnitude of their contributions. They still enlarge our understanding of the process through the dark night of the soul, where godliness in character and vision are forged. Most of us cannot expect our voices to hold such significance for subsequent generations, but their example can encourage us as we seek to be faithful to God's work in and through our own lives.

The Power of Your Utterance

To have a voice is to have a say in something. The way we use the word *voice* provides clues to the ways we instinctively view its meaning. We say, "The president has lost his voice over this matter," or "My university professor was a key voice in my life," or "John the Baptist was a voice crying in the wilderness."

To voice something is to articulate opinions, ideas and truths. To be a voice is to influence others through one's personal identity and strength of expression. When your voice speaks, the power of your utterance affects others through declaration, expression, pronunciation, proclamation or enunciation. In the Hebrew, the translation of the word *voice* is related to the terms *declaration* and *proclamation*, and also to the verb *prophesy*.

A person's voice articulates words, and words possess power and authority. A person's voice also incorporates his or her personality and character. In other words, a voice is not only what is said, but it is also the power and authority that lie behind what is said. Voices create something. Voices connect back to the source of their authority, which in our case is God Himself.

The most influential voice comes from someone who has a pure heart and who therefore can articulate what God is saying clearly (see Psalm 24:3–4). Such a voice stands in God's place as he or she expresses words out loud. Jesus said the pure in heart will see God (see Matthew 5:8). Then they will say what they see.

Your God-Given Identity

To be an effective voice in the Kingdom of God, you and I must know two things: (1) who God is, and (2) what our unique identity is.

116

Three components form your awareness of your unique identity. At the deepest level, you are what you know about yourself in your innermost self, what you know about your thoughts, feelings, secret desires, strengths, weaknesses and dreams. Others do not know that part of you unless you tell them.

A second component of your identity is who other people think you are. You cannot know that part unless they tell you. People who do not know what others think of them have a void in their self-awareness. You do not know all there is to know about who you are if others do not communicate to you how they see you. That is one reason relationships with family, friends and community are so important. We need others to tell us how they see us, so we can come to know ourselves more fully through that information.

Only God knows the third component of your identity. He will show you over time, through revelation. He will uncover His mind, showing you whom He created you to be. One way this occurs is through the prophetic Voice of God, either through others or directly to you in your communication with Him.

The Simple Power of a Voice

While mulling over the simple power of a voice in a person's life, I thought about my childhood experiences with my father and mother. I loved both of them dearly. They were each unique, and they each had their own way of approaching things. My distinct experiences with them as individuals help me understand the concept of voice, because by nature they each had a unique voice. Let me explain by telling you a little bit about myself.

I was one of those children whom parents hope they are ready for. If they had only known in advance that someone like me was on the way, they could have gone on a forty-day fast and called for help! I was a handful. I got into anything that looked different and interesting. I felt compelled to find anything that was hidden. I had to pursue anything that was challenging. I had to overcome anything that I had been told was impossible. Being told *not* to do something was to me an invitation to do that very same thing. I was a boundary pusher, always probing for a way to go farther. I hated boxes; I considered them something to break out of.

Why did I come equipped with that kind of personality? God created me to have a unique voice! He wanted that voice to propel me into my calling. My personality as a child was the seed that emerged over time into the fullness of my mature voice.

My parents were given a voice to set my course for the future. I remember that when I was about five years old, my mother dressed me up in one of those snowsuits that resembled a mummy's wrap. It was big, bulky and wrapped tight, like the snowsuit in the movie *The Christmas Story*. Then she sent me outside to play. From our house, I wandered across the street, through a park-like area, to a small pond surrounded by bushes and trees.

When I reached the edge of the pond, I just had to step out and walk on the ice covering the pond. Why? Because for starters, I was Barbara. But I was also captivated by the goldfish under the ice. I loved those giant goldfish! I just had to see them close up. I thought it fascinating that those big orange fish were swimming under the ice in the wintertime. They were not even frozen. I had thought everything froze solid in the winter.

Out onto the ice I tiptoed. Suddenly the ice began to crack, and then it gave way. I found myself slipping down into the water with a shriek, frightened to death. I was a hostage of my snowsuit, helpless. I tried to find a way to escape. I kept grabbing at the shelf of ice, but each time, another piece broke off. Each time, I slipped back into the water a little more, until finally only my head was peeping out. I could not move in my snowsuit, and the wet ice was too slippery for me to get any kind of grip on it. I knew I was going to drown. Besides that, I knew my mother would be really mad. I was not supposed to go to the pond by myself.

It was either drown for sure or yell for help (never mind the consequences from my mother). So I began yelling extremely loudly! Finally, someone heard my hollering and ran to pull me to safety. Had it not been for this passerby, I probably would have drowned.

Needless to say, when my rescuer took me home, Mother was distraught. But nothing she could say, even with me still shivering in front of her, could have made me heed her earlier warnings. Why is that? Because she had a very limited voice with me. No, I do not mean a case of chronic laryngitis—the problem was that she had fretted and fussed over me so often before that I did not take her seriously anymore. I might just try the same dumb thing next time I went outside because I had learned to ignore her warnings.

Every day, Mother chased me around, telling me to stop this or stop that. She tried desperately to bring me into order. She found the willow switch and chased me down with it so often that I had became accustomed to that game, and I had become deaf to her threats because of the frequency with which she raised her voice. I did not enjoy being shouted at, of course; I found it downright disparaging. Yet it did not motivate me to change because I did not respect it.

Now, I loved my mother. I always wanted her nearby when I was sick or hurting or in some kind of emotional distress. I did *not* want her around when I was pushing boundaries, though. Her voice brought me comfort, emotional support and that warm, fuzzy feeling when I needed it, but her voice did not have any effect on my otherwise challenging behavior. My mother's voice spoke into only one part of my formation.

Then there was my father. I never remember him ever raising his voice to me. He certainly did not chase me around. He never said a bad word to me, nor did he ever have a bad word to say about anyone. He was a stable, steadying type of person, and he had a "presence." He was a dignified man, a confident man whose quiet and wise demeanor commanded both respect and authority, not only in our home but also in the larger community.

All Dad had to do was *look* at me and I knew what he was saying. His *voice*, his very presence, commanded my attention even when he did not say a thing. He did not have to chase me around, yell at me or spank me. He could simply look at me and quietly tell me what to do, and immediately I would jump to fulfill his request. For him, I stopped my antics. Without his word and corresponding presence, I would have grown up self-willed in the extreme, hard to manage for the rest of my life. Dad was a major voice in my life.

My mother was not a bad mother. Everyone loved her. However, she possessed a completely different voice and presence than my father. For some reason, she lacked something when it came to having a voice that a child would recognize as one to be reckoned with. My father did not even have to try, however. His authoritative voice was simply part of his persona, and all of us submitted to it. My father's voice alone could create whatever order was needed in our household. It was love combined with firmness. He did not need to turn up the volume, because volume had nothing to do with it. His voice had both the power and the requisite authority to create order and to establish obedience and respect.

The Purpose of the Voice

Consider the voice of John the Baptist. The Bible tells us that he was a voice crying in the wilderness, and the message of his voice was, "Prepare the way of the LORD; make His paths straight" (Matthew 3:3).

The purpose of John's voice was to announce the new thing God was beginning to do. In the midst of darkness, John declared what would be happening. He declared what would occur to transform the dark night into a bright morning of visitation, filled with the power and presence of God. John proclaimed that something would come out of nothing. He saw in the midst of the wilderness what God was going to do. He envisioned what was coming, even though it did not yet exist.

"John the Baptist came as a voice crying in the wilderness." We repeat that powerful statement without thinking about it. This time pause and think about it. The *wilderness*—that is where John came from. He was not repenting. He was not weary or confused. John was lifting up his voice. He was thundering, shouting aloud and calling out. He was proclaiming, apprehending through words, pronouncing, prophesying—out of the wilderness.

If you and I are to penetrate the wilderness and darkness, we have to learn to cry out in our own way. The wilderness will always be the hardest place to cry out from. But if you and I do not first cry out with our voice in the wilderness, the new day will not be formed and the light will not come into the midst of darkness. Transformation will never occur.

The wilderness is our solitary place, our lonesome wasteland, our desolate, empty space, wherever our course of action is uncharted and our way is unclear. "Crying" out means to proclaim publicly, to announce, declare, state, make known, decree, assert, broadcast or pronounce. By raising our voices, we are publishing or heralding a message.

This crying out from the wilderness and darkness is not a quiet conversation. It is a confrontation. It is also a prophetic pronouncement and declaration, the origin of which does not lie within you or me as individuals, but with God. Our crying out is God speaking through us. Our voices echo His Voice within us.

The Voice Is a Word of Declaration

Before things happen, prior to their coming into being, they must be *declared*. This declaration must precede the completion of something that has been coming into fullness in some way. It is a prophetic function, because prophecy is partly foretelling. The voice or prophecy authoritatively declares what will occur. Isaiah declared, "See, the former things have taken place, and new things I declare; before they spring into being I announce them to you" (Isaiah 42:9, NIV).

So the prophetic voice prepares the way by informing us that something is going to change. The purpose of the voice is to create vigilance in the hearers as well as in the speakers. Furthermore, it infuses faith into a situation. It makes people watchful, aware, expectant, alert. They both watch for and watch over, through informed intercession, what is about to unfold. The prophetic voice causes them to expectantly take action to prepare a place for the working out of the declared word in real time.

The prophetic voice does not focus on the enormity of the task as much as it focuses on the all-sufficiency of God:

Abraham didn't focus on his own impotence and say, "It's hopeless. This hundred-year-old body could never father a child." Nor did he survey Sarah's decades of infertility and give up. He didn't tiptoe around God's promise asking cautiously skeptical questions. He plunged into the promise and came up strong, ready for God, sure that God would make good on what he had said. That's why it is said, "Abraham was declared fit before God by trusting God to set him right." But it's not just Abraham; it's also us! The same thing gets said about us when we embrace and believe the One who brought Jesus to life when the conditions were equally hopeless. The sacrificed Jesus made us fit for God, set us right with God.

Romans 4:19–25, MESSAGE

The Voice Is a Word of Preparation

You can liken the function of the voice to what happens when a baby is in its mother's womb. The doctor's voice has announced that a baby is there. The mother's physical form is changing. She is altering and adjusting her feelings, expectations and actions to something new. At the right time, that new baby (the new thing) arrives. The new parents have made preparations, and a new structure is in place—they have set aside a room and made it ready for the newborn; they have purchased clothes, formula and diapers. The voice that declared what would come to pass has helped prepare the way. Life is about to change drastically. The new parents have come to the end of life as they have known it, because a new life is coming into their home.

The Voice Is Powerful

The voice cries out in the empty place and declares that something new is about to come and fill up that emptiness. The voice responds to prophetic insight and revelation from the Holy Spirit in words, dreams and visions. The verb *voice* means to call aloud, sound out, shout or proclaim. It is not soft and quiet—the voice thunders, releasing a sound that by its very nature is authoritative, powerful and even loud.

Now that you understand the meanings of *voice* and its numerous effects, consider the phrase "the voice of the LORD" in Psalm 29. (I have italicized the word *voice* in the psalm for the purpose of emphasis.)

> The *voice* of the LORD is over the waters;
>> the God of glory thunders,
>> the LORD thunders over the mighty waters.
> The *voice* of the LORD is powerful;
>> the *voice* of the LORD is majestic.
> The *voice* of the LORD breaks the cedars;
>> the LORD breaks in pieces the cedars of Lebanon.
> He makes Lebanon skip like a calf,
>> Sirion like a young wild ox.
> The *voice* of the LORD strikes
>> with flashes of lightning.
> The *voice* of the LORD shakes the desert;
>> the LORD shakes the Desert of Kadesh.
> The *voice* of the LORD twists the oaks
>> and strips the forests bare.
> And in his temple all cry, "Glory!"
>
> Psalm 29:3–9, NIV

This Scripture captures the power of God's Voice or word to situations. It is authoritative and commanding, causing things to happen, to come into existence and change. I love the phrase "the voice of the Lord strikes with flashes of lightning." Suddenly things may change because God releases His Voice, His word, into a situation.

The Voice Cries Out

Since John the Baptist was a voice "crying" in the wilderness, does this mean that he was weeping copiously? Was he travailing, with tears and much emotion? Not necessarily. It means he had a compelling message, a word from God, something that was supposed to arrest, to apprehend and to capture the heart of the hearers. His crying was a creative and powerful declaration of the message of his *voice*.

Such crying can have a personal aspect to it. The "crier" can accost someone and call out his or her name. The cry of the voice may be addressed to a specific person, people, situation or even a specific geographical place—by name. Remember how Jesus cried out to Jerusalem?

> O Jerusalem, Jerusalem, the one who kills the prophets and stones those who are sent to her! How often I wanted to gather your children together, as a hen gathers her chicks under her wings, but you were not willing! See! Your house is left to you desolate; for I say to you, you shall see Me no more till you say, "Blessed is He who comes in the name of the LORD!"
>
> Matthew 23:37–39

Prepare the Way of the Lord

Your voice, which is distinct to you personally and is enhanced by God's work in your life, is meant to announce the coming of the Lord Jesus into every place your feet (or your prayers) may take you. Each of us has a different assignment. If we say yes to our assignment, we can expect to receive "voice lessons" for the rest of our earthly life.

One way I received voice lessons was through learning to recognize that when people and situations come to my mind, God is alerting me to things I need to be aware of. (Really the awareness comes to my spirit, but I recognize it as my mind because I perceive it as a thought.) So I learned to begin contacting these people and praying for them and for the situations concerning them. Paying attention to and acting on these alerts is one of the ways I have learned to pastor God's people. Often God gives me an interventional impression that, when I put it into words, becomes His Voice in the situation, transforming the spiritual environment and infusing it with faith. Exercising my voice for Him in this way has been a major focus of my "voice lessons."

How have you been exercising your voice? Have the hardships of the dark night season in which you have been immersed silenced it? Or have you been able to break out with cries of declaration, proclamation and preparation for the new day that lies ahead of you?

Just as John the Baptist cried out from the wilderness, so can you. By crying out, you prepare the way for the Lord Himself, Lord Sabaoth, so that He can enter into and transform not only your own dark wilderness, but also the wilderness of the world that lies at your doorstep. He will come to you with His new overcomer's anointing, ready to prepare you for whatever lies ahead.

9

Your Forerunner Anointing

You are powerful. You are significant. God has given you a voice. He has given you a passion for Himself. He has given you a heart. He has created something inside you that is drawing you into a place you have never been before. A desperation for God is growing in your heart. You are part of what some leaders are calling "the saints movement," in which ordinary believers become a powerful force in the earth.

God wants His Voice to thunder through common, ordinary people. He wants His Voice to go into hospitals and heal the sick. He wants His Voice to speak a transformational word of deliverance to alcoholics and drug addicts. He wants His Voice to transform ghettos and to change and lift up the spirits of people in the inner city. He wants to affect Wall Street, the White House, governmental offices, corporate headquarters, CEOs and scientists.

His Voice—coming through us, simple, ordinary people—
cries out in the middle of desolate places. It declares the word
of the Lord, the will and the heart of God to people in all of
these places. A simple, ordinary person's voice can go anywhere
it is sent. Directed by the Lord, such a voice is powerful. Such
a voice penetrates defenses and goes to the heart of the issue,
transforming people and situations.

What would happen if you believed that your voice is that
powerful? What if you would become a voice for Him in the
world today? What if the reason God allowed you to pass
through your dark night was to strengthen and reinforce your
belief in Him, so that you would believe that His Voice through
you is mighty and that He can and will help you persevere
through the most impossible situations victoriously?

We Are Forerunners

Your voice and mine are meant to combine. It is part of our
call that is reminiscent of the call of John the Baptist, the call
to be a forerunner—one who runs before, announcing the ad-
vent of someone or something new. A forerunner goes before
something new to prepare the way. A forerunner is prophetic,
as Isaiah expressed:

> Pass through, pass through the gates!
> Prepare the way for the people.
> Build up, build up the highway!
> Remove the stones.
> Raise a banner for the nations.
>
> Isaiah 62:10, NIV

> A voice of one calling:
> "In the desert prepare
> the way for the LORD;
> make straight in the wilderness

a highway for our God.
Every valley shall be raised up,
 every mountain and hill made low;
the rough ground shall become level,
 the rugged places a plain.
And the glory of the LORD will be revealed,
 and all mankind together will see it.
 For the mouth of the LORD has spoken."
A voice says, "Cry out."
 And I said, "What shall I cry?"

Isaiah 40:3–6, NIV

A forerunner clears the way for the apostolic builders and intercessory "maintenance workers." A forerunner may also help build the new thing and be earnest in prayer. A forerunner comprehends the vital importance of having one's *voice* formed and framed by the Holy Spirit Himself, the One who hovers over darkness until it is transformed into the new day. A forerunner is called to seek alignment with the Holy Spirit.

Remember what happened to Lucifer when he defied the will of God in heaven and introduced another will that was against that one will? Do not underestimate the weight of aligning your will with God's will in order to proclaim His rule into the new day.

You cannot consider the power of the voice without understanding alignment. The key verse in the New Testament regarding alignment is found in the eleventh chapter of Hebrews: "By faith we understand that the worlds were *framed* by the word of God, so that the things which are seen were not made of things which are visible" (Hebrews 11:3, emphasis added).

Note that the key word is *framed*. It is important to see that the apostle Paul does not use the word *make* or *create* here. He writes that worlds were *framed* by God's Voice, which means that they were aligned with His intentions.

In the Greek, the word translated as "framed" is *katartizo*. The word means "to put in order, to arrange, to complete—to align." Framing is related to creation, but the idea is that the already-created elements are adjusted or arranged into order, or fitted together harmoniously.

The point of all this talk about alignment is that we can align things through our words—which are prophetic declarations if they match up with God's will—and that thereby we can participate in the creation of the new moment, new time, new opportunity or new order. The author of our words is God. Aligned with the Spirit, we are expressing His will. We are verbalizing His intentions.

Forerunners change the flow of history. Our voices can echo God's Voice, when His mantle or anointing falls on us. When His anointing comes, a boldness comes with it. Our voice speaks out, saying, "It's going this way. Shift over here." Our voice does not back off. It tackles each structure that blocks the way. It dismantles it, layer by layer, and gets to the core of the matter. It dismantles the old framework, and then it methodically creates, layer by layer, line upon line, a new arrangement.

Ezekiel declared the word of the Lord to dry bones, and they revived into a mighty, conquering army (see Ezekiel 37). His voice had power because it was so perfectly aligned with God's word and God's will. "For with God nothing is ever impossible and no word from God shall be without power or impossible of fulfillment" (Luke 1:37, AMP).

In the Spirit of Elijah

Jesus said, "For all the prophets and the law prophesied until John. And if you are willing to receive it, he is Elijah who is to come" (Matthew 11:13–14). Did He mean that Elijah had already come? Or that Elijah was yet to come? Who is Elijah in this context?

In this passage, Jesus was referring to another coming of Elijah. Before Jesus comes again in a new and fresh way, a prophetic company will arise to prophesy and declare what God is going to do. They will come in a reconciling spirit to restore fathers and children. They will come and miraculously prepare the way in the new place by prophesying and declaring what is to come. The spirit of the forerunner we talked about, John the Baptist, is the spirit of Elijah:

> See, I will send you the prophet Elijah before that great and dreadful day of the LORD comes. He will turn the hearts of the fathers to their children, and the hearts of the children to their fathers; or else I will come and strike the land with a curse.
>
> Malachi 4:5–6, NIV

So in becoming someone who is like John, one who is a voice in the wilderness, we carry a John the Baptist anointing and an Elijah mantle. Such a voice shakes systems and works miracles. Such a voice is born after the Spirit of God takes a person off into the wilderness. Part of the responsibility of such a voice is to turn situations, organizations, times, seasons and people toward God. You and I, in the spirit of John the Baptist and Elijah, are supposed to turn things. We have a turning ministry.

You may be saying, "But I am an ordinary person." Even so, your voice has the power to turn things in an extraordinary way, miraculously.

A New Heart of Compassion

Now that you have come through your dark night, you can become a fresh, new voice to those who are passing through their own dark nights, those who are in the valley of the shadow of death or those who have no answers for the challenges they face.

You have faced the worst, so you can now arise with faith for dire situations in your church, in cities, in states or in nations. What you have passed through has given you understanding and compassion for anyone else captured by darkness—whether they are Islamic, Buddhist, Hindu, New Age, atheists, agnostics, those disillusioned by their life experiences or those turned off by their experiences in the Church or with Christians. You cannot do for others what you have not faced yourself, but having faced the darkness, your voice can speak into the darkness of others.

The Power of Pentecost

The power of Pentecost is that when the Holy Spirit came upon 120 ordinary disciples in the Upper Room, they did not stay in that room and nurse their new experience. They ran outside those four walls, into the midst of the city of Jerusalem, and began proclaiming what they had seen and experienced. They became a voice. That voice was able to speak into the lives of people from multiple nations and life situations. Those who heard that voice were changed by God, and in turn they changed the cities and nations from which they had come.

So often we have settled for an experience and then nursed the experience instead of fulfilling the purpose of the experience. We have driven our tent pegs down into the ground and contained the voice in one place. Yet that voice the disciples were given was meant not only to go into Jerusalem (the city), but it was to go into Judea (the state), Samaria (the nation) and to the uttermost parts of the earth (see Acts 1:8). Their voice was a power in the earth, designed to transform the world and the people who heard it.

Taking It to the Streets

Recently while eating in a restaurant, I engaged the young woman waiting on our table in conversation. I asked her about herself: What had brought her to my town? Where was she from? What was her major in college?

The whole time we conversed, I silently prayed, asking God if there was something He wanted me to tell her. I began to be aware that her heart had been broken. Looking at her, I gently mentioned that God knew about the sore in her heart. Tears welled up in her eyes, and she blurted out, "How did you know? I've tried to keep it hidden!" I explained to her that God loved her so much that He cared about that hurt in her heart—so He showed me it was there. She began to cry. I told her about God's heart for her and about His love and longing to heal her heart and set her free. Finally, I helped her make her way to the bathroom, where she could wash her tear-stained face in cold water and regain control so she could finish out her shift.

That night was the start of an ongoing relationship with that student. She has not yet found her way to healing, but my voice expressed God's Voice to her that night so that her desolate heart could grab hold of a ray of hope. I believe our God is a God who can invade the earth with His power and His presence, and when we understand who He is, He literally overcomes us. Just as you and I were overcome when we finally believed, it is just that easy for people to believe and be overcome today.

I am convinced that when people and situations spiral downward into darkness, you and I ought not be overwhelmed. In one sense, we need to get excited. That sounds strange. However, biblically, as darkness gets darker, the light must become lighter!

God's Word says that when darkness descends, our light has come and the glory of the Lord will arise upon us:

ARISE [from the depression and prostration in which circumstances have kept you—rise to a new life]! Shine (be radiant with the glory of the Lord), for your light has come, and the glory of the Lord has risen upon you!

For behold, darkness shall cover the earth, and dense darkness [all] peoples, but the Lord shall arise upon you [O Jerusalem], and His glory shall be seen on you.

Isaiah 60:1–2, AMP

Turning on the Light

A Light is coming. When that Light comes, our faces will shine like the face of Moses. Even though you have always been an ordinary person, after the anointing of God's glory comes upon you, the people who come near to you will see the light and glory of the Lord. Your life in Christ will become visible. Others will see the change; some will tell you what they now see in you.

God gave these now-familiar words to Isaiah the prophet: "The former things have come to pass, and new things I declare" (Isaiah 42:9). What does that mean in your life? Let me give you one example from mine. I live in an economically depressed state. I believe God has assigned me to this state. I am called to be part of the answer, not part of the problem or a victim of the circumstances. It is dark here. Yet it is not too dark for me to understand that I am called to be a voice that proclaims a fresh, new way in the midst of darkness and desolation.

I believe that I can tap into God's Voice, and then release my voice to creatively birth new ideas, innovations, businesses and endeavors that can and will transform this state's economy. This is not unprecedented. Even when Israel was under Egyptian bondage, the Israelites flourished because they obeyed God's Voice through Moses. Isaac prospered in a time of famine because he obeyed the word of the Lord. Later, Jacob flourished in lean times because he entered into God's provision through his son Joseph. The Voice led them all to a place of prosperity in the midst of decline. God has intentionally assigned us to live in the midst of darkness so that we can be co-redeemers with Him.

Our voices, echoing His Voice, rearrange and repair the messes around us. Our words have the power to align heaven with earth and vice versa. They have the power to align *kairos* time, creating opportunities for transformation. *Kairos* times are windows of opportunity that are time limited but strategic and life changing, whether that life is a person's or a city's. When a *kairos* time occurs, we need to attend to it immediately because of its time-limited nature. A window opens, and then it closes. Consider the tragedy of 9/11. Many people opened up to God for a season because they had no answers for the magnitude of the tragedy. That season of openness was a *kairos* time in their lives, time limited but life changing for many.

God's Voice is life-giving. "Thus it is written, The first man Adam became a living being (an individual personality); the last Adam (Christ) became a life-giving Spirit [restoring the dead to life]" (1 Corinthians 15:45, AMP). The Voice brings back to life people and things that have died.

God's Voice is also faith-imparting; it conceives and brings forth. It can come in dreams of the night or in visions. It can come while you are writing in your journal. His Voice can come through a prophetic word, a word of knowledge or a word of wisdom. The One who spoke into the darkness and said "Let there be light" is imparting His constructive Spirit to you and me, and He is showing us how to step out of our temporary dark night into the light of the new day.

He has called you and me as forerunner voices in the lives of those with whom we intersect. We are to speak His clear word into their desolate, chaotic, empty places and let our voices release hope and vision for the future.

It is the same today as it was in the beginning of the Bible. Without leaving our assigned places in our families, jobs and neighborhoods, we can become agents of miraculous change, voicing His will and releasing His light into a world that is out of order and broken. A world so lost in darkness seems beyond repair. But even the darkness is light to Him. That is why He can take our darkest hours and turn them into our greatest spiritual weapons. Nothing is impossible with Him.

10

The Inextinguishable Light

My new condo, built into a low hillside and beautifully landscaped, was my private refuge. I felt so safe there, and I enjoyed the pastoral scene outside my floor-to-ceiling windows.

Late one warm night, I had just crawled into bed. Dropping off to sleep, I jolted wide awake when I thought I heard a rustling in the bushes. There was a thump on my window. Somebody had pushed his way through the thick bushes and was now standing right in front of those triple, floor-to-ceiling bedroom windows. I lay in total darkness, staring at this shadow of a human figure through the closed blinds. The streetlights from above outlined the person's upper torso.

My heart was thumping so loudly that it seemed whoever was out there would hear it. I could see that I had left the middle window wedged open. I did not think the intruder could climb through it because of its narrow width. Yet it was open. What should I do? What could I do?

In the pitch-black room, my eyes fell on the illuminated dial of my telephone. I grabbed the phone and pulled the covers up over my head to muffle my voice and block the phone's light from view. Quickly, I dialed 911. By the time the police arrived, the person had escaped. After talking with the officers, I shut and locked the window, returned to bed and lay awake for a very long time.

The next morning, it dawned on me that one tiny light on a telephone dial had made all the difference. I thought of John 1:5: "And the Light shines on in the darkness, for the darkness has never overpowered it [put it out or absorbed it or appropriated it]" (AMP). One tiny gleam of light could not be hidden by the thick darkness. It had been a beacon of deliverance to me.

God's Light: A Beacon of Deliverance

God never lets His light go out. In the midst of our darkness, He makes sure that a light shines forth. It may be a song, a Scripture, a person or a word spoken at just the right time. Never will God leave us without hope. Your darkness may be gut-wrenching, nail-biting, sheer hanging-on-by-a-thread trust in what the Bible declares is true. The darkness may seem as thick as it was for the people of Israel in Egypt. Nevertheless, the light in the midst of the darkness cannot be extinguished. If it does not come in the form of a pillar of fire, it may come in the form of a telephone keypad, as it did for me.

Years ago as a young Christian, I was going through a trying time. During one early morning moment of half sleep, half wakefulness, God spoke a word to my heart. It was so clear that I sat straight up. "When He has tried me, I shall come forth as gold." Unexpectedly, in the midst of that difficult time, there came that word. It was a light in the midst of darkness to guide my feet through a dark place. It framed my expectations in a new way. Because of that word, I knew that my difficulty would not go on forever and that after a short while, my trial would be over. Because of that word, I knew how to posture myself. Through the trial, God was working something in my character. If I allowed Him to change my character, I would come forth a richer person. When God was finished, the situation would fade away. That word was a light in the midst of darkness.

Light in the Darkest Night

Jesus, the Light of the world, could never be overcome, even by the darkest night that anyone ever faced. In His final days on earth, however, Jesus came to a place where it looked like it was all over.

First, there was Judas. He was one of those twelve disciples who knew Jesus best. Judas had been with Jesus for over three years, had eaten with Him, slept in the same quarters with Him and dialogued with Him. Judas had left his old life to follow the Rabbi from Nazareth. Then that same Judas betrayed Jesus for money, handing Him over to His accusers. Who would have believed such a thing could happen?

Has anyone ever betrayed you, walked out on you, dissed you? This was the ultimate betrayal. And after Judas betrayed Him, Jesus was abandoned by the other eleven disciples, captured by the authorities and put on trial. His adversaries succeeded in winning a guilty verdict. The sentence for Him was death on a cross. Where was the light now?

Jesus trudged up the hill, carrying that heavy cross onto which they nailed Him. Strangers stood by and mocked Him, asking, "Who is this? The King of the Jews?" Ultimate humiliation! He hung there, bleeding and panting, for what seemed an eternity. The life was draining out of Him. Empty, without strength to go on, totally wrung out from the depths of suffering, despairing of life itself, some words slipped out of Jesus' mouth. Mary heard them, and so did the others standing nearby. Out of the depths of utter darkness, He cried out, "My God, My God, why have You forsaken Me?" (Matthew 27:46; Mark 15:34). Shortly thereafter, He died.

Though it was midday, even the daylight slipped through Jesus' fingers. That day turned into darkest night. Now Jesus was a prisoner of darkness, ultimate darkness, death itself. Satan, the lord of death and darkness, had overcome Him—so it seemed. For all anyone knew, it was over. All the earth shook with an enormous earthquake; graves were opened; the dead released. This was no ordinary death.

Nevertheless, Jesus was dead. Dead and gone, seemingly to be erased from time and history. The women gathered around the tomb. They had prepared Jesus for burial. They had handled His dead body, which was now in the windowless, unlighted chamber behind the stone, entombed in darkness, shrouded in death. Both Marys were there, one sitting by the tomb. What were they thinking? Probably, *How could this be?* Darkness enshrouded them, too, like a burial cloth. The One they loved was gone. It was over!

As if to add to the finality, Pilate assigned armed guards to the tomb. He wanted to make sure that nothing happened, that no one would steal Jesus' body and then claim He had risen.

The women joined the disciples, mourning behind closed doors in the city. Three long days and nights passed, seeming more like one endless night. Nobody thought about tomorrow. Nobody thought about today. Hope had expired along with their Lord, Jesus.

Nothing Can Extinguish the Light

Suddenly, what was this? Another earthquake rumbled the city. An angel of the Lord appeared at the entrance of the tomb.

He took one look at the giant stone and rolled it away. This angelic being, mighty in power, magnificent in bearing, was cloaked in lightning, the brightness of God's glory. His light outshone the rays of the early morning sunshine. He came boldly to announce, through his actions, that nothing could put out the Light of the world. Even death could not entomb Jesus, who was bigger than death, mightier than any chains of bondage. He was Life itself. Nothing could hold Him captive. The angel told the women who had come once more to the tomb, "He has risen from the dead! He is alive. He has gone before you into Galilee. Go find Him, He is waiting for you" (see Matthew 28:7).

What jubilation! Such unbelievable news! Ecstatic joy! Jesus alive—risen from the dead! The women were beside themselves. They raced to tell the disciples.

The long night was over. They had thought that Jesus' life was over, but no; it was the other way around. It was death and darkness that were over—they had failed to hold Jesus in their grip. Nothing, not anything, could extinguish the Light of the world, who was Jesus. It was impossible for death to hold the trump card. Jesus would always have the final word. And Jesus' word was the Word of Life and Light:

> From the very first day, we were there, taking it all in—we heard it with our own ears, saw it with our own eyes, verified it with our own hands. The Word of Life appeared right before our eyes; we saw it happen! And now we're telling you in most sober prose that what we witnessed was, incredibly, this: The infinite Life of God himself took shape before us.
>
> We saw it, we heard it, and now we're telling you so you can experience it along with us, this experience of communion with the Father and his Son, Jesus Christ. Our motive for writing is simply this: We want you to enjoy this, too. Your joy will double our joy!

This, in essence, is the message we heard from Christ and are passing on to you: God is light, pure light; there's not a trace of darkness in him.

1 John 1:1–5, MESSAGE

The Light can never be extinguished, overcome, defeated, overpowered, mastered, apprehended or held hostage. The Light shines in the midst of darkness, and darkness cannot overwhelm it. The Light pierces the darkness and uncovers the hidden and secret places. Nothing can remain hidden once the Light shows up.

The Message: Light Prevails

This is the incredible message to you and me personally in every place—geographical, physical, mental, emotional, spiritual—in every circumstance, relationship or assignment: When we belong to the Light of the world, no darkness, no evil strategy, no force set against us can ultimately overpower us. The Light of the world always shines out in the midst of darkness. Neither darkness nor death can hold it—or hold us—hostage. Therefore fear cannot rule us. The God who has claimed us as His own is more powerful than any darkness, even the darkness of death.

This is our message: Though it seems that darkness and death may be overtaking us, they can never extinguish the Light of the world, Jesus Christ. If we merely align ourselves with Him, He will break us all the way through any barriers. Nothing can stop Him. With Him, we will overcome!

The Light will keep shining until the darkness is overcome. God will send a word or a vision, and it will be enough to keep us going all the way through the long night, even if it turns into our longest night on record. Remember Joshua and Caleb?

They had to wait out 45 years of complaints from their fellow Israelites, but they persevered. Not only did they persevere, but they remained healthy and strong, well able to enter the land that God had promised them. Here are Caleb's words:

> The Lord has kept me alive, as He said, these forty-five years since the Lord spoke this word to Moses, while the Israelites wandered in the wilderness; and now, behold, I am this day eighty-five years old.
>
> Yet I am as strong today as I was the day Moses sent me; as my strength was then, so is my strength now for war and to go out and to come in.
>
> So now give me this hill country of which the Lord spoke that day. For you heard then how the [giantlike] Anakim were there and that the cities were great and fortified; if the Lord will be with me, I shall drive them out just as the Lord said.
>
> Then Joshua blessed him and gave Hebron to Caleb son of Jephunneh for an inheritance.
>
> So Hebron became the inheritance of Caleb the son of Jephunneh the Kenizzite to this day, because he wholly followed the Lord, the God of Israel.
>
> Joshua 14:10–14, AMP

Caleb would not let go of what God had said. That promise was an unextinguishable light to him in the midst of every dark place. It was the word of God Himself, released prophetically to Caleb's heart.

Many times I have received what seemed to me huge, overwhelming, seemingly impossible assignments from the Lord. Yet I accepted them, knowing that God through Jesus Christ would anoint me to overcome all odds. If He has given me a charge, then it is within my grasp to fulfill it, because it is His assignment, not mine.

This is true for each one of us—*if* we remain His. What does that entail? These important things:

Build on the foundation of Jesus Christ. First, we must make sure that the sole foundation on which we build our lives is God alone! Not money, success, position, fame or anything other than God and His Word. Paul told Timothy that the foundation of the Lord is sure (see 2 Timothy 2:19). It is certain, definite, immovable, steadfast and secure. It does not change.

Obey in every detail. Second, are we doing what God has told us to do? Have we taken on the right assignment? If we have, no matter how difficult it gets, we *will* overcome. One of God's names is *Jehovah Nissi*, which means "God our Banner." *Jehovah Nissi* revealed Himself when the Israelites defeated the Amalekites (see Exodus 17:15). Overwhelmed with the odds, Joshua went into battle while Moses stood on top of the mountain, with Aaron and Hur holding up his arms. As long as they all did what God had told them to do, the victory was theirs. After persevering together, they overcame.

When you are doing what God has told you to do, you should never, never, never give up! Though all of hell may array itself against you (and it will), you cannot lose if you follow God. His Light can never be extinguished. Somehow you will overcome everything that is set against you if you commit for the long haul and not just for the moment.

I have pastored for many years. Many times it has looked like my church was going down for the count. Yet, as in Carman's dramatization *The Champion*, though we were often almost out, at the last moment, the eleventh hour—oftentimes it seemed like it was past time—victory came. Knocked down, we have never been knocked out.

Surround yourself with the right people. Third, are we carrying out our assignment with the people God told us to do it with? This, too, requires attentiveness on our part. What if someone turns out to be a "bad apple"? Will that void the contract?

No, not if that person was someone assigned to you. Jesus had a traitor named Judas in His group. Judas was assigned to Him. So Jesus moved forward for three years with a potential traitor in His strategic group of twelve. In spite of (and, ironically, in some ways because of) Judas's actions, Jesus overcame death. Through the betrayal, Judas positioned Jesus for His greatest triumph. And Jesus fulfilled His destiny, His mission. He gathered those whom His Father had told Him to gather, and the rest was up to God. Jesus did not put His trust in His men, but He taught them how to trust in God. The rest of Jesus' disciples ended up carrying this message to the world.

Take decisive action in a timely manner. Fourth, are we moving out when God tells us to move? I watch many people receive a word of the Lord instructing them to take action. However, they wait until it is convenient. Or they analyze it out of existence. They interpret God's direction in light of their schedules. God is never convenient, but He is always on time. Waiting until it is convenient for us is moving God's initiatives into our world, our power. We end up shooting ourselves in the foot.

When God tells you to take action *now*, then do it! The strategic time to move will not wait for you. Timing is everything. Seizing the moment is critical. The right moment, seized, will transform itself into momentum. When momentum begins to build, stay with it.

Recently I was in a situation where nothing looked hopeful, not even minutely so. Yet God told me to move out and begin to declare what He had said. There were no signs whatsoever of light in the midst of this darkness. Nevertheless, I obeyed God and began to declare what He had instructed me to declare. Miraculous intervention began to break out, slowly at first. Then as others in the situation began to take note, they changed their actions, and suddenly the whole situation began to turn around. Attitudes changed, hearts changed, minds changed. People's words began to line up with what God was saying. Suddenly, though the situation had looked totally bleak, a complete turnaround occurred.

Could it be that you are in just such a time? With the darkness of circumstances surrounding you, everything in you wants to quit, give up, stop walking in midstep. Yet you cannot forget what God said. No matter how bad it gets, you cannot get His word out of your head. Grab hold of it; do not let go! Get up today whether you feel like it or not. Move forward! Declare the truth. You *will* overcome. You *will* break through. Your destiny is assured if you wholeheartedly follow the Lord.

He Must Win the Battle

We are in the direst of times. My nation and many others sit teetering on the brink of financial collapse. Public confidence in the authority systems of government and business corporations is at an all-time low. Many Christians seem to have lost their way. Everything is a mess.

Yet, in the midst of all this, a Light is arising. The glory of the Lord is the greatest where the darkness is the most intense (see Isaiah 60:1–2). Genesis 1:2 frames our paradigm for how to view confusing, contradictory, messy times. It shows us how it is the chaotic messes that attract the brooding, hovering attention of the Holy Spirit. In other words, because we are in a mess, *we qualify for some divine intervention*!

Though desperation abounds in the world, this is the Church's day. We have an opportunity to influence the nations we live in positively. How can we possibly shift an entire state, a province or a whole nation? By concerted, unified prayer and strategic, God-directed intervention.

In my own state of Michigan, we defined a thirty-five-day period immediately before the national election in 2008 (right on top of the breakout of the Wall Street crisis). We prayed together at 6:00 A.M. (the break of day), so that we could command the day. We called for pastors, churches, intercessory groups, houses of prayer, Christian businesses, governmental prayer groups, families and individuals across Michigan to pray every morning for one hour starting at 6:00 A.M., because of the critical *kairos* time at hand not only for Michigan but for our nation. We started on September 30, 2008, because it was the beginning of the Jewish biblical New Year. To establish this as part of the new, we wanted to enter not just a new year but also a new era. We called it forth and declared a season of breakthrough on many fronts: the economy, the government, churches, families and individuals.

The day before our September 30 beginning, the Dow fell by 777 points. Did you catch the significance of that? Three sevens on that day! The number seven represents the end of a cycle, and the number three represents the Trinity, so it was as if God said, "I am ending this Myself." I believe it represents God's perfect judgment on man's system. When God begins to bring order out of chaos, foundations that He cannot bless always come under His judgment. You can expect to see judgment escalate, by the way, not just outside the Church, but also inside the Church. Do not be intimidated or fearful as you see corporations, governments, banking institutions, schools and even churches seemingly fall apart. At the breaking of day, God makes a way in the uncharted territory that appears to be a hopeless mess (see Isaiah 43:18–21).

Align with What God Is Doing

As the new day dawns in the middle of the current chaos, you and I need to remind ourselves of these important ways we can align ourselves with what God is doing:

- Do not be afraid or intimidated by what seems to be falling apart, because God is putting His Church in place.
- Do not try to hold the old things in place. God is dismantling them.
- Resist the temptation to fix anything that can no longer be fixed.
- Close out, shut down, exit those activities, programs or efforts that God is no longer blessing and you have been struggling to continue.
- Listen and watch for God's presence. Where is He? Watch for the wind of God's Spirit. Catch that wind, for it will take you to the new place.

As we pay close attention to what God is doing right now, more and more light dawns in us and around us. Matthew 6:22–34 (MESSAGE) says,

Your eyes are windows into your body. If you open your eyes wide in wonder and belief, your body fills up with light. If you live squinty-eyed in greed and distrust, your body is a dank cellar. If you pull the blinds on your windows, what a dark life you will have! . . .

If you decide for God, living a life of God-worship, it follows that you don't fuss about what's on the table at mealtimes or whether the clothes in your closet are in fashion. . . .

Instead of looking at the fashions, walk out into the fields and look at the wildflowers. They never primp or shop, but have you ever seen color and design quite like it? . . .

If God gives such attention to the appearance of wildflowers—most of which are never even seen—don't you think he'll attend to you, take pride in you, do his best for you? What I'm trying to do here is to get you to relax . . .

Give your entire attention to what God is doing right now, and don't get worked up about what may or may not happen tomorrow. God will help you deal with whatever hard things come up when the time comes.

We are in an extremely pressing time, but also an extremely exciting time. It is a time to celebrate, to rejoice. God's grace is coming in an unusual and remarkable way. Paul said that God's grace is sufficient. Keep praying. Keep looking for the Light that is shining steadily in the midst of the swirling darkness.

Keep saying what God is saying, because God has begun to take action. He has heard our prayers, and He is answering. In the middle of the night, the Church is arising with a light that cannot be extinguished, and dawn is just around the corner.

Overcoming Power

Martin Luther faced formidable religious powers when he nailed his ninety-five theses to the church door in Wittenberg, Germany. He got his prerequisites right—his foundation was built on Christ alone, his timing was good and the specifics of what he did and whom he allied himself with were appropriate. The momentum his boldness created led to the Reformation, a remarkable turning point in the history of Christianity. Martin Luther carried a light that overcame the tyranny of religious oppression and heresy. He initiated the beginning of the restoration of truth to the Church. Through his experiences of facing down the darkest of religious spirits, he crafted one of the greatest hymns of the church, "A Mighty Fortress Is Our God":

> A mighty fortress is our God, a bulwark never failing;
> Our helper He, amid the flood of mortal ills,
> prevailing:
> For still our ancient foe doth seek to work us woe;

His craft and power are great, and, armed with cruel
    hate,
On earth is not his equal.

Did we in our own strength confide, our striving
    would be losing;
Were not the right Man on our side, the Man of God's
    own choosing:
Dost ask who that may be? Christ Jesus, it is He;
Lord Sabaoth, His Name, from age to age the same,
And He must win the battle.

And though this world, with devils filled, should
    threaten to undo us,
We will not fear, for God hath willed His truth to tri-
    umph through us:
The Prince of Darkness grim, we tremble not for him;
His rage we can endure, for lo, his doom is sure,
One little word shall fell him.

That word above all earthly powers, no thanks to them,
    abideth;
The Spirit and the gifts are ours through Him Who
    with us sideth:
Let goods and kindred go, this mortal life also;
The body they may kill: God's truth abideth still,
His kingdom is forever.

May this hymn become your testimony. You, too, have been
given a light that shines in the darkest of places. The prince
of darkness *is* grim. But you and I do not need to tremble because of his rage. With "one little word"—a God-sent, exacting
word—we can cause his purposes to fail.

Not only will that one little word from God thrust the
enemy through, it is that word from God that will transform
you from a coward to an anointed overcomer. In that one

word from God, you will find your anointing for overcoming the darkness. Why? Because it will activate—in fact, it will ignite—your faith. That word will then frame your actions and transform your situation, and suddenly you will break through the darkest of circumstances. That word will be transformed from a word heard to a word fulfilled. Now you have a "word of testimony." You have overcome, causing Satan's plan to fail. And you cannot help but tell everyone about it. Your test has become your testimony because of one little word.

> And they have overcome (conquered) him by means of the blood of the Lamb and by the utterance of their testimony, for they did not love and cling to life even when faced with death [holding their lives cheap till they had to die for their witnessing].
>
> Revelation 12:11, AMP

> They defeated him through the blood of the Lamb
>   and the bold word of their witness.
> They weren't in love with themselves;
>   they were willing to die for Christ.
>
> Revelation 12:11, MESSAGE

That utterance of their testimony, that bold word of their witness, is the declaration of the saints who experienced God's overcoming work through His revelatory word made flesh in them. His word was exerted in and through them to overcome. One more time together, let's recall what 2 Peter 1:19 (AMP) says about the prophetic word:

> And we have the prophetic word [made] firmer still. You will do well to pay close attention to it as to a lamp shining in a dismal (squalid and dark) place, until the day breaks through

[the gloom] and the Morning Star rises (comes into being) in your hearts.

The Word of God will hold you steady until the breaking of the new day. It will happen. The day will break through the gloom of any present darkness. If you believe the Word and persevere, God will use your darkest hour as your greatest spiritual weapon. You will overcome. Receive God's overcoming anointing now!

Afterword

We have now entered the most challenging time we have ever faced. World systems are shaking; in fact, they seem to be falling apart. All the things people have looked to, depended on, valued and esteemed are no longer what they once were. As globalization increases, change is escalating at a pace we can barely keep up with. Traditional institutions are suddenly crashing to the ground overnight. Nations take over and exchange banking systems and economies; governments merge; some countries decline and others emerge into positions of importance.

Everything that can be shaken will continue to shake in this day. The shaking will intensify to the point that most people will cry out for an answer to the questions, Where is the solid ground? Where is the Kingdom that cannot be shaken? How do we unite with that which does not shake—God's Kingdom—and come out from a world system that will keep shaking until it shatters?

God is dealing not only with us individually, but with the kingdoms of this world. The same process that applies to an individual entering a new day—passing through the dark night of the soul, coming out of the old day and coming into the new—applies to families, to neighborhoods, to churches, to cities and ultimately to nations. God's dealings will intensify to the end, all the way from an individual level to a worldwide scale, because what is being shaken out at every level needs to make way for the new, the one Kingdom that can never be shaken, God's Kingdom:

> Unlike your ancestors, you didn't come to Mount Sinai—all that volcanic blaze and earthshaking rumble—to hear God speak. The earsplitting words and soul-shaking message terrified them and they begged him to stop. When they heard the words—"If an animal touches the Mountain, it's as good as dead"—they were afraid to move. Even Moses was terrified.
>
> No, that's not your experience at all. You've come to Mount Zion, the city where the living God resides. The invisible Jerusalem is populated by throngs of festive angels and Christian citizens. It is the city where God is Judge, with judgments that make us just. You've come to Jesus, who presents us with a new covenant, a fresh charter from God. He is the Mediator of this covenant. The murder of Jesus, unlike Abel's—a homicide that cried out for vengeance—became a proclamation of grace.
>
> So don't turn a deaf ear to these gracious words. If those who ignored earthly warnings didn't get away with it, what will happen to us if we turn our backs on heavenly warnings? His voice that time shook the earth to its foundations; this time—he's told us this quite plainly—he'll also rock the heavens: "One last shaking, from top to bottom, stem to stern." The phrase "one last shaking" means a thorough housecleaning, getting rid of all the historical and religious junk so that the unshakable essentials stand clear and uncluttered.

Do you see what we've got? An unshakable kingdom! And do you see how thankful we must be? Not only thankful, but brimming with worship, deeply reverent before God. For God is not an indifferent bystander. He's actively cleaning house, torching all that needs to burn, and he won't quit until it's all cleansed. God himself is Fire!

Hebrews 12:18–29, MESSAGE

It is for such a time as this that God has called you. It is why you entered the dark night of the soul and withstood its onslaughts, allowing God to remove from you that which needed removing so you could finally break through to a new day. Whether your dark night is now over or whether you are still going through it, the purpose of the process is to forge a whole new understanding in your mind and heart.

Now you know, not only for yourself but also for other individuals and even for entire nations, that "dark times" are God's opportunity to initiate His grand new day, the emergence of His Kingdom, which will stand forever. As He enters your world and the world to transform the night into a whole new day, do not resist what is transpiring. Stand back, worship and let God direct you as you walk with Him into the new thing He is doing today, both in your personal life and in world systems.

Notes

Chapter 1: The Challenge of Darkness

1. Robert Stearns, "The God Who Hides in Darkness," *KAIROS*, May/June 2008, 12.

2. Elie Wiesel, *After the Darkness: Reflections on the Holocaust* (New York: Schocken Books, 2002), 5.

Chapter 2: Behold, I Do a New Thing

1. Dave Sim, quoted at http://thinkexist.com/quotes/dave_sim/.

Chapter 3: The God Who Is Light

1. David Yonke, "A Hollywood Plot Twist: *Basic Instinct* Author Writes Book about Faith," *Toledo Blade*, August 23, 2008, posted at http://toledoblade.com/apps/pbcs.dll/article?AID=/20080823/NEWS10/808230343.

2. Ibid.

Chapter 4: The Breaking of the New Day

1. St. John of the Cross, *Dark Night of the Soul*, Book II, Chapter 9, Section 1.

2. Chuck D. Pierce, *God's Unfolding Battle Plan* (Ventura, Calif.: Regal Books, 2007), 101–2.

3. In my book *The Breaker Anointing*, I wrote extensively about the gate, the threshold and the narrow place that accompany going through to a new place. See Barbara J. Yoder, *The Breaker Anointing* (Ventura, Calif.: Regal Books, 2004), 43–67.

4. Pierce, *God's Unfolding Battle Plan*, 102.

5. Mario Murillo, *Critical Mass* (Port Bolivar, Tex.: Anthony Douglas Publishing, 1985).

6. Words by Sir John Bowring (1792–1872). Public domain.

Chapter 5: God's Heart for Restoration

1. Charles Colson with Anne Morse, "My Soul's Dark Night," *Christianity Today*, December 2005, posted at http://www.christianitytoday.com/ct/2005/december/15.80.html.

2. Ibid., emphasis added.

3. Sally Pobojewski, "The First 21 Days," *Medicine at Michigan* 10 (Spring 2008): 25, posted at http://www.medicineatmichigan.org/magazine/2008/spring/21days.

4. Os Hillman, "The Black Hole," TGIF [Today God Is First] Daily Workplace Inspiration internet series, February 6, 2004, posted at http://www.marketplaceleaders.org/apps/articles/default.asp?articleid=4825&columnid=744.

Chapter 6: The Battle of Wills

1. For a much more detailed understanding of who Lucifer was and is, see Donald Grey Barnhouse, *The Invisible War* (Grand Rapids: Zondervan, 1965).

2. Bob DiCesare, "Kisabeth Went Long for TD Catch," *Buffalo News*, August 29, 2009, posted at http://www.buffalonews.com/sports/story/425741.html.

Chapter 7: The Struggle to Believe

1. Os Guinness, *God in the Dark* (Wheaton: Crossway, 1996), 23.

2. Ibid., 23–25.

Chapter 8: The Voice

1. Stephen R. Covey, *The 8th Habit: From Effectiveness to Greatness* (New York: Free Press, 2004), 87.

2. Ibid., 5, 85.

3. Ibid., 24.

Barbara J. Yoder is senior pastor and lead apostle of Shekinah Christian Church in Ann Arbor, Michigan. Shekinah is an apostolic and prophetic church with a multiracial, multicultural constituency. Barbara believes the Church must engage God's presence to see the release of God's breakthrough power, which affects and ultimately transforms both people and territories locally, regionally and internationally. She puts a strong value on the centrality of the presence of God, the Word, prayer and worship in the life of the Church. She believes the Church is not a building but a people, called to move out of the four walls and into the marketplace (government, business, education), with a passion to transform the world, one person at a time. And she never forgets that Jesus loved people and was called a friend of sinners.

Barbara has also mobilized a developing network of churches and ministry leaders called Breakthrough Apostolic Ministries Network (BAM). BAM has four divisions that equip, train and support leaders of local churches, leaders in business and government, intercessory leaders and leaders of ministries. She has an emerging call to business and government leaders for the purpose of transformation—supporting them in releasing the Kingdom of God in the marketplace, as well as developing new paradigms and nurturing an innovative atmosphere that enables them to change with the times and seasons.

A third endeavor of Barbara's is Breakthrough Leadership Institute, a regional school with the purpose of equipping and training individuals to fulfill their call not only in the Church but also in the marketplace. Barbara believes that the core anointing of an apostolic people is breakthrough, enabling them to overcome every hindrance and obstacle, thereby ushering in God's transforming power. Further, the strategic release of breakthrough knowledge, power and wisdom must arise out of a prophetic heart and spirit.

Barbara has an abiding passion to connect with likeminded leaders across regions, states and nations. Above all, Barbara has a passion for God, for people and for life, which has been forged out of years of experience with both the triumphs and challenges of real life. Through it all, she has learned to value realness, and she believes that an untested Christian life that has not come through difficulties victoriously lacks genuineness. In addition to *The Overcomer's Anointing*, other books Barbara has authored to help people grow into the fullness of who they are in Christ include *The Breaker Anointing*, *God's Bold Call to Women* and *Taking On Goliath*.

For more information about Shekinah Christian Church, BAM and Breakthrough Leadership Institute, as well as other resources available from Barbara J. Yoder, visit www.shekinah church.org. To contact Barbara, write or call:

Shekinah Christian Church
P.O. Box 2485
Ann Arbor, Michigan 48106
Telephone: (734) 662-6040
Fax: (734) 662-5470
Email: pastorbarbara@shekinahchurch.org